FOR ORGANS, PIANOS & ELECTRONIC KEYBOARDS

7

3rd Edition

Hits from Musicals

ISBN: 978-1-4234-1051-5

HAL•LEONARD®
CORPORATION
7777 W. BLUEMOUND RD. P.O. BOX 13819 MILWAUKEE, WI 53213

As Long as He Needs Me
from the Broadway Musical OLIVER!

Registration 1
Rhythm: Fox Trot or Swing

Words and Music by
Lionel Bart

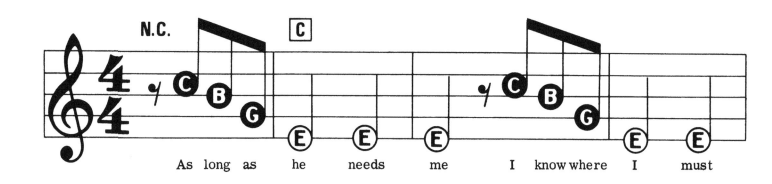

As long as he needs me I know where I must

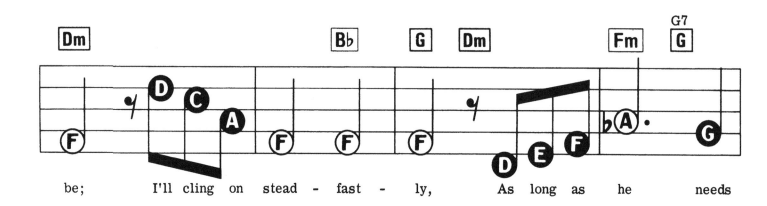

be; I'll cling on stead - fast - ly, As long as he needs

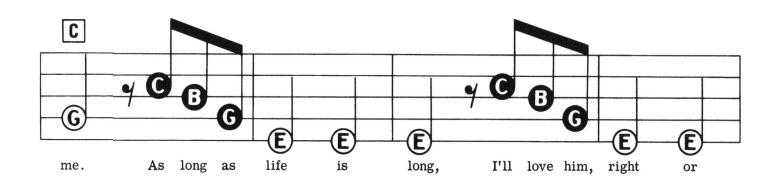

me. As long as life is long, I'll love him, right or

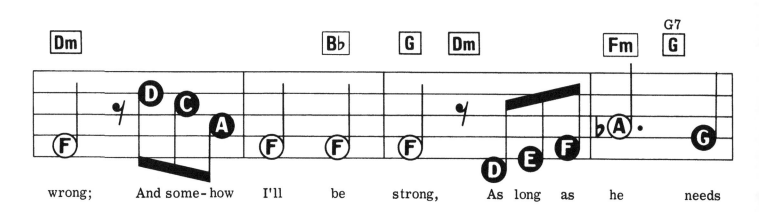

wrong; And some-how I'll be strong, As long as he needs

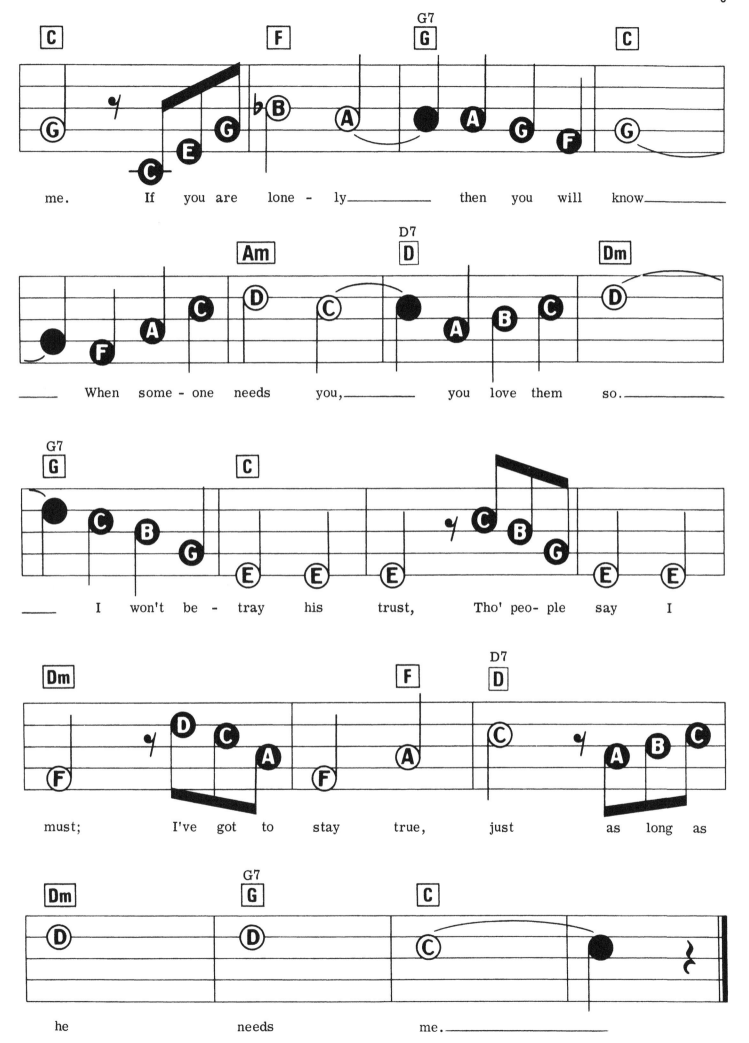

Day by Day
from the Musical GODSPELL

Registration 2
Rhythm: Rock or 8-Beat

Music by Stephen Schwartz
Lyrics by Richard of Chichester (1197-1253)

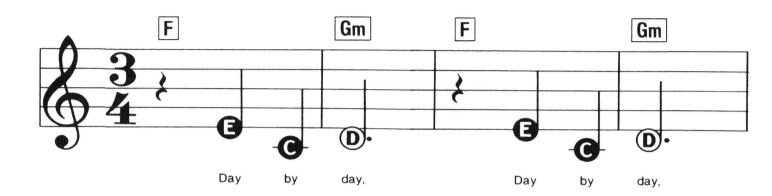

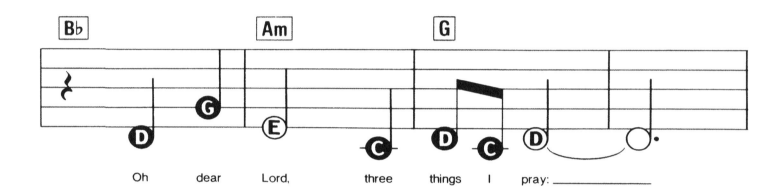

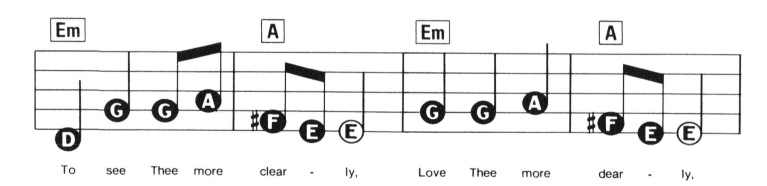

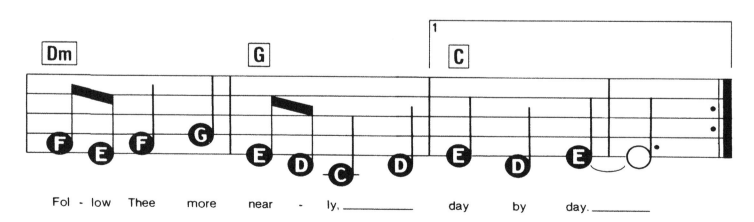

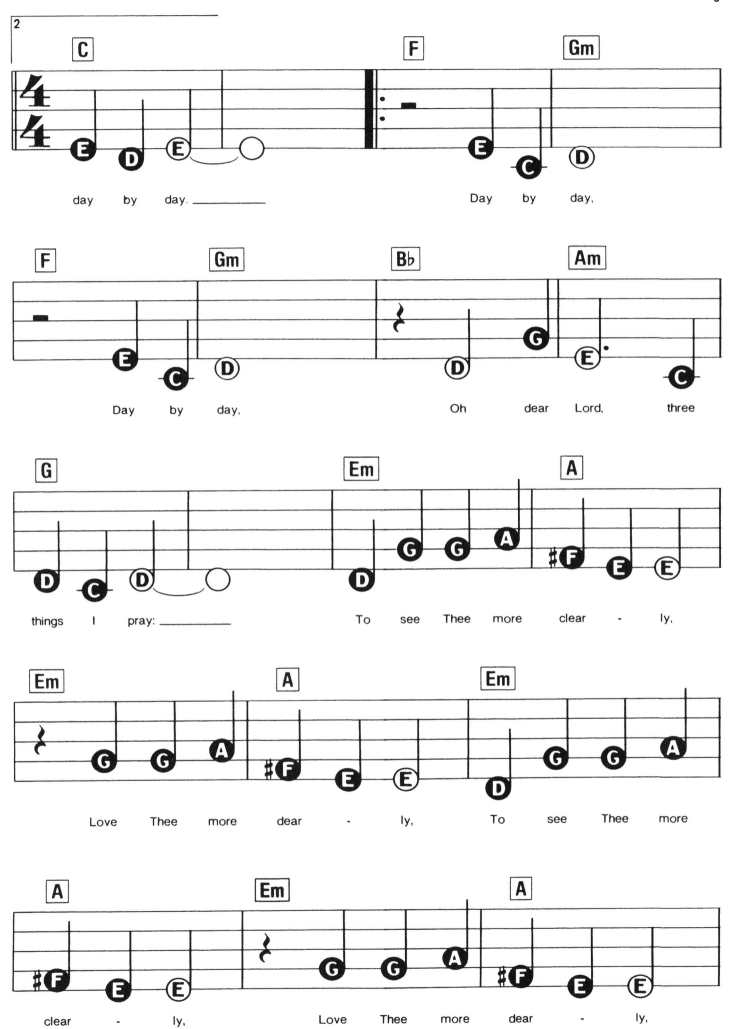

6

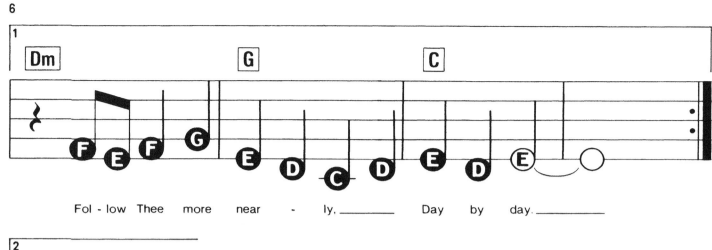

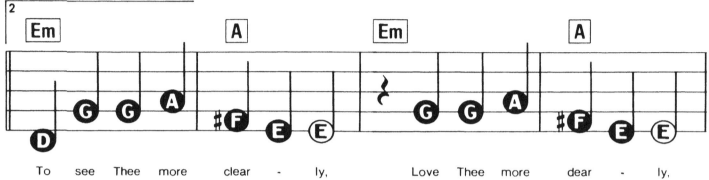

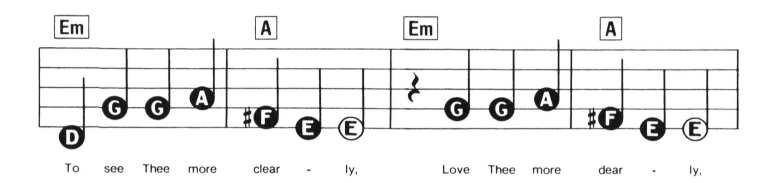

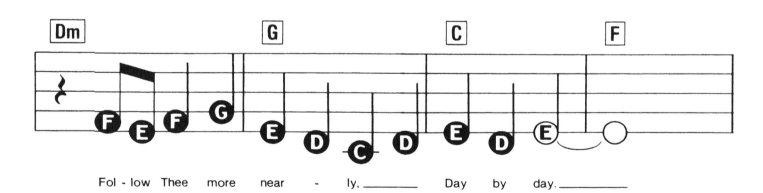

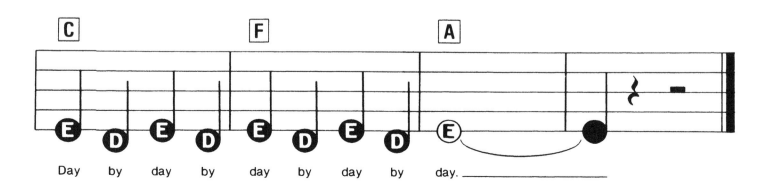

She Loves Me
from SHE LOVES ME

Registration 9
Rhythm: Rhumba

Words by Sheldon Harnick
Music by Jerry Bock

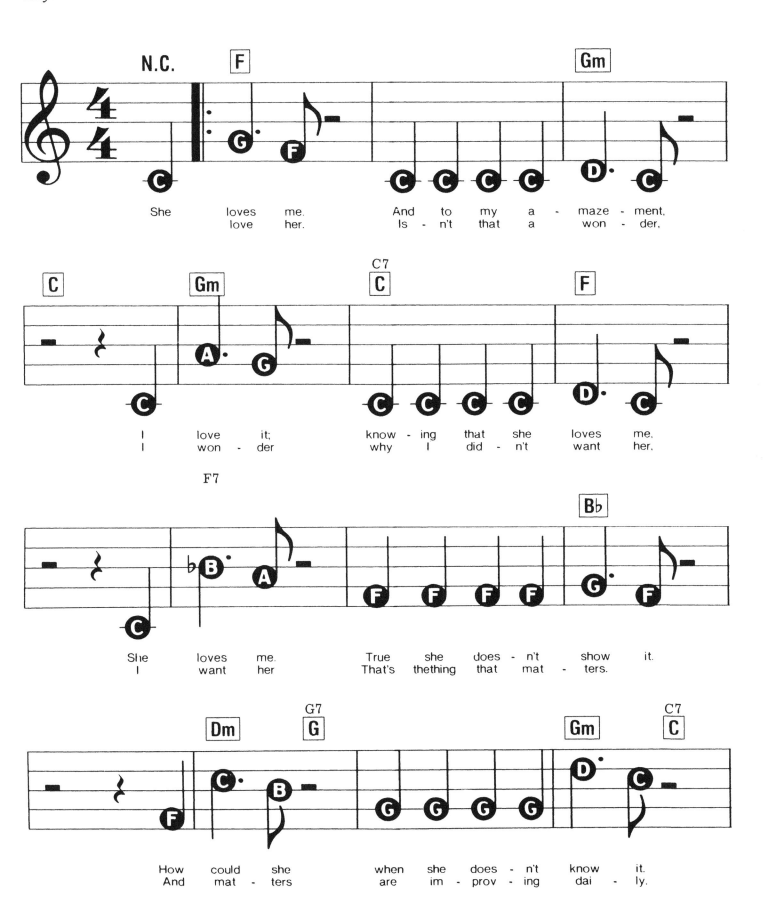

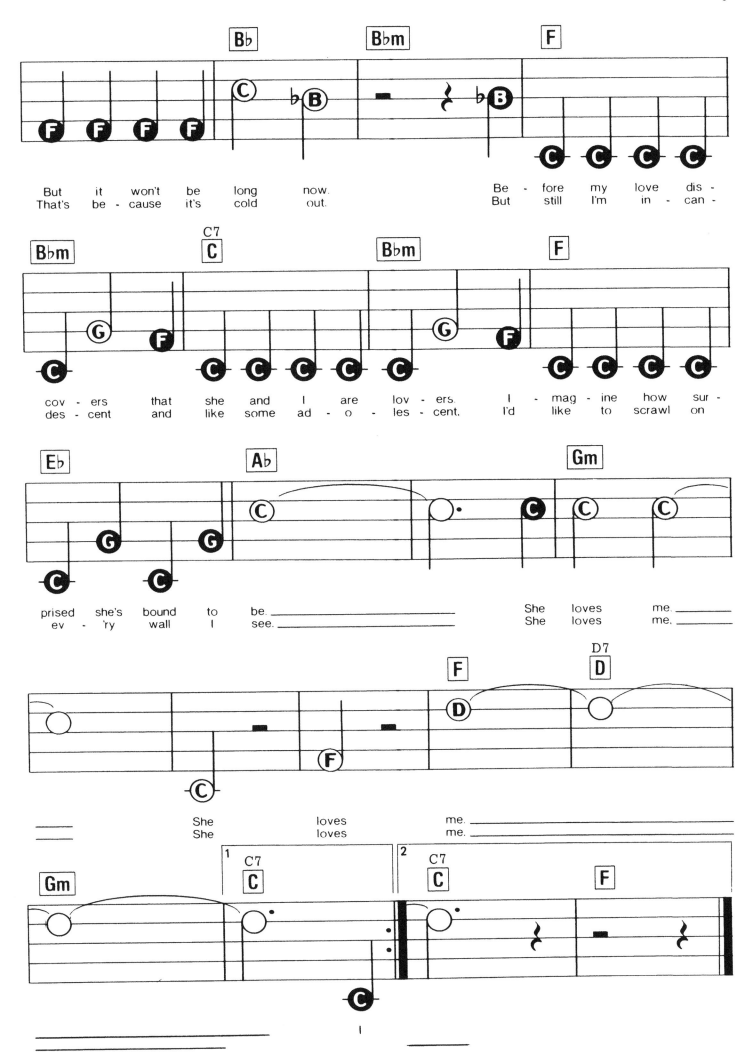

Falling in Love with Love

from THE BOYS FROM SYRACUSE

Registration 5
Rhythm: Waltz

Words by Lorenz Hart
Music by Richard Rodgers

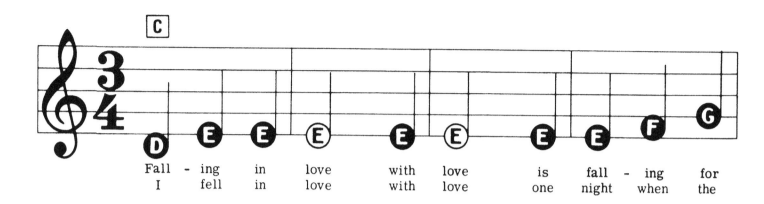

Fall - ing in love with love is fall - ing for
I fell in love with love is one night when the

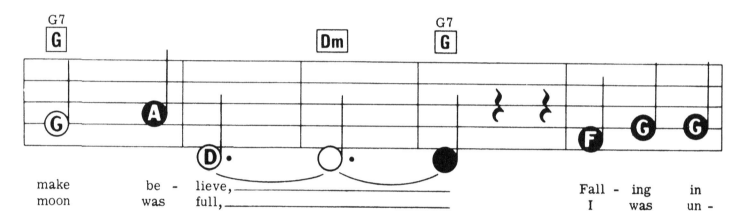

make be - lieve,_____ Fall - ing in
moon was full,_____ I was un -

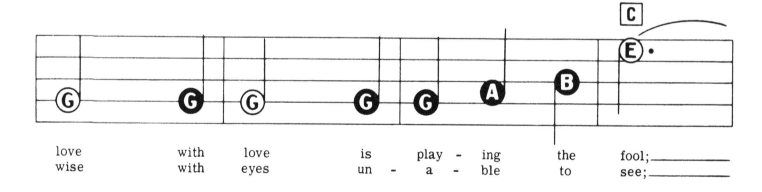

love with love is play - ing the fool;_____
wise with eyes un - a - ble to see;_____

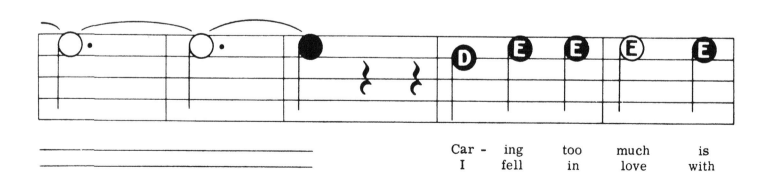

Car - ing too much is
I fell in love with

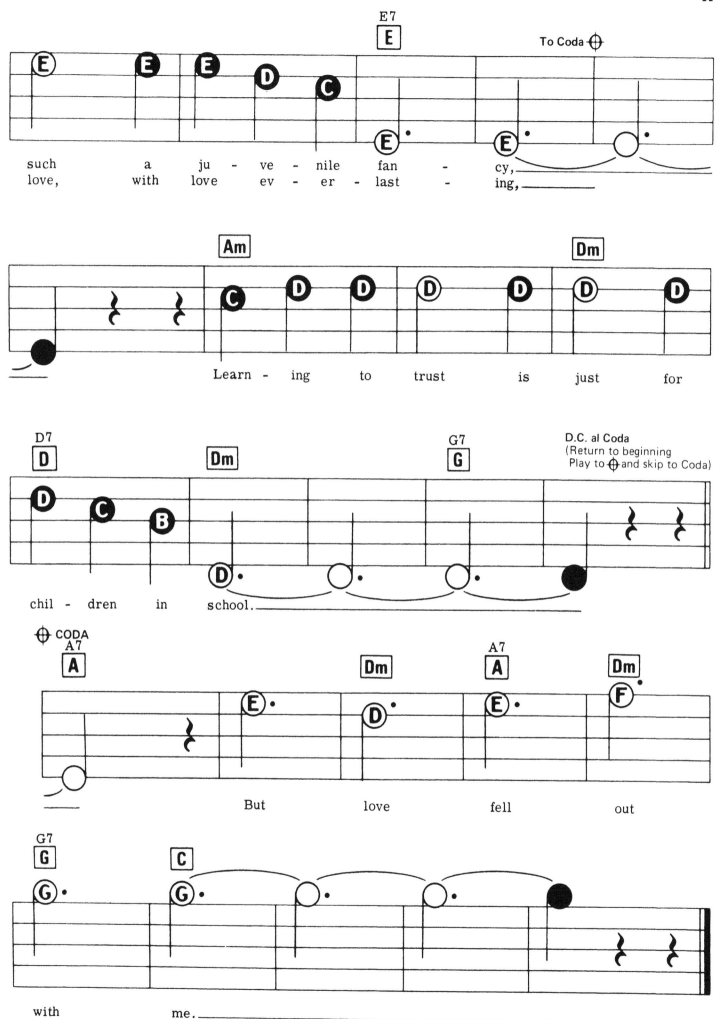

Gonna Build a Mountain
from the Musical Production STOP THE WORLD - I WANT TO GET OFF

Registration 4
Rhythm: Fox Trot

Words and Music by Leslie Bricusse
and Anthony Newley

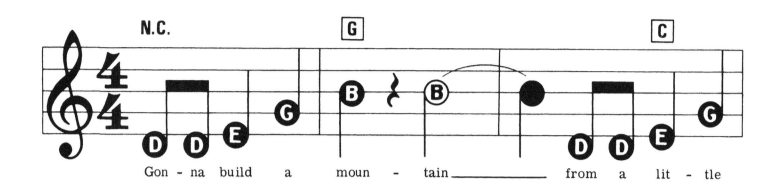

Gon - na build a moun - tain ____ from a lit - tle

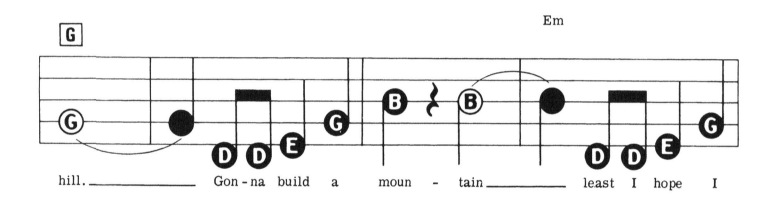

hill. ____ Gon - na build a moun - tain ____ least I hope I

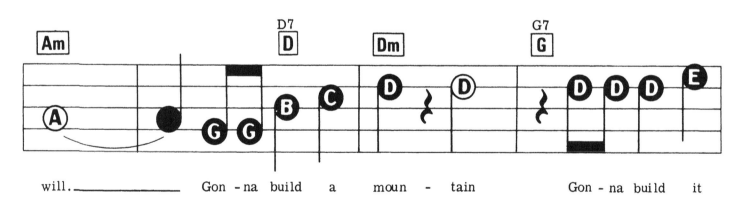

will. ____ Gon - na build a moun - tain Gon - na build it

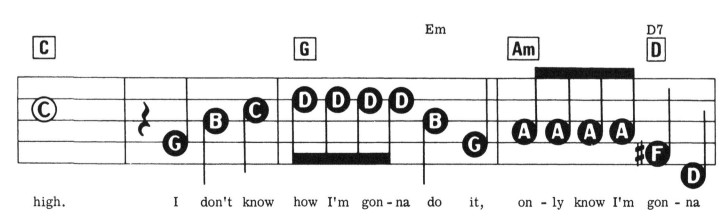

high. I don't know how I'm gon - na do it, on - ly know I'm gon - na

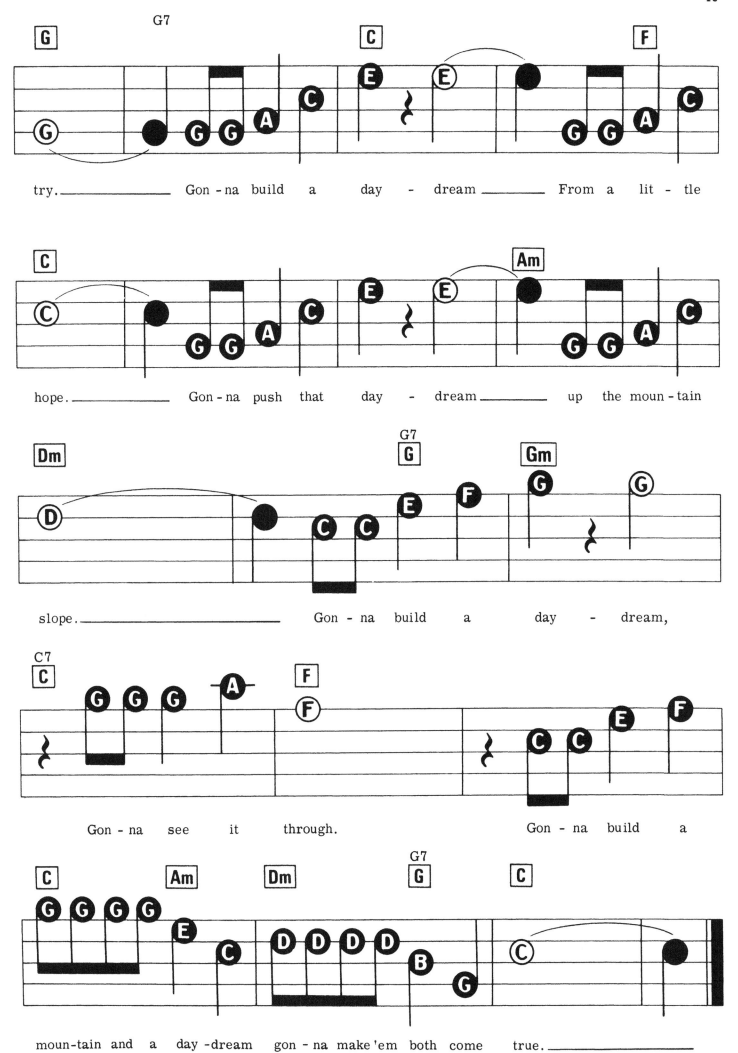

Hello, Dolly!

from HELLO, DOLLY!

Registration 5
Rhythm: Swing

Music and Lyric by
Jerry Herman

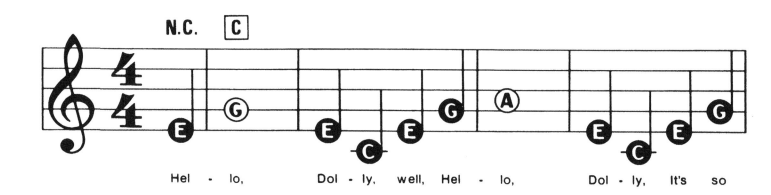

Hel - lo, Dol - ly, well, Hel - lo, Dol - ly, It's so

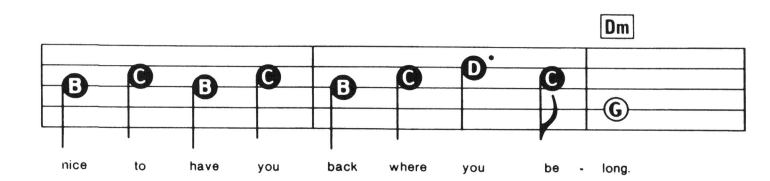

nice to have you back where you be - long.

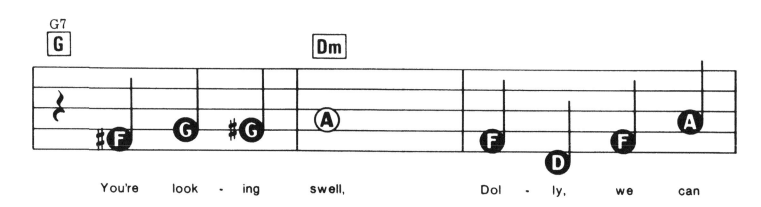

You're look - ing swell, Dol - ly, we can

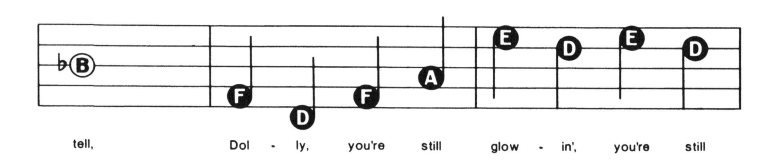

tell, Dol - ly, you're still glow - in', you're still

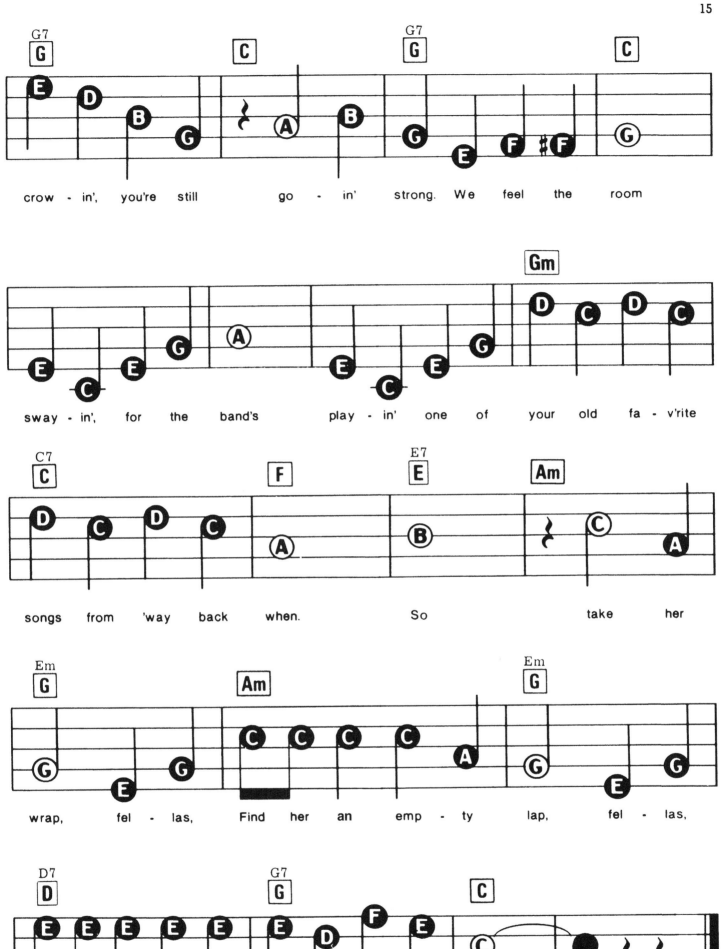

I Could Write a Book
from PAL JOEY

Registration 7
Rhythm: Fox Trot or Swing

Words by Lorenz Hart
Music by Richard Rodgers

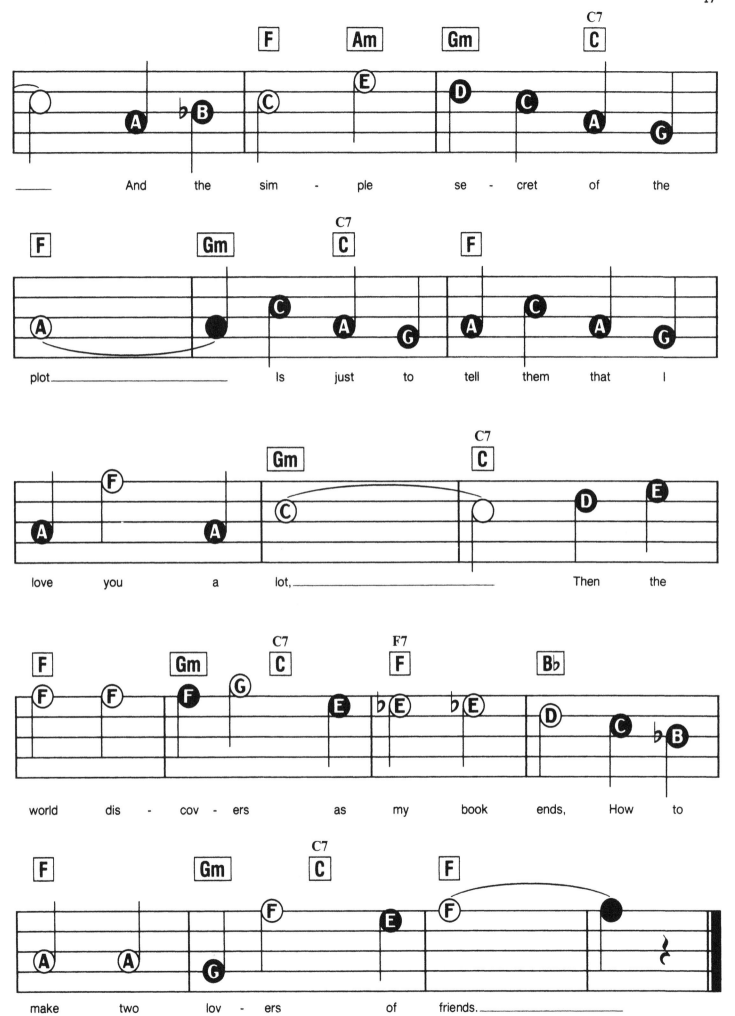

I Dreamed a Dream
from LES MISÉRABLES

Registration 1
Rhythm: Ballad

Music by Claude-Michel Schönberg
Lyrics by Alain Boublil, Jean-Marc Natel and Herbert Kretzmer

I dreamed a dream in time gone by
He slept a sum - mer by my side.

when hope was high and life worth liv - ing.
He filled my days with end - less won - der.

I dreamed that love would nev - er die.
He took my child - hood in his stride.

I dreamed that God would be for - giv - ing.

Then I was young and un - a - fraid.

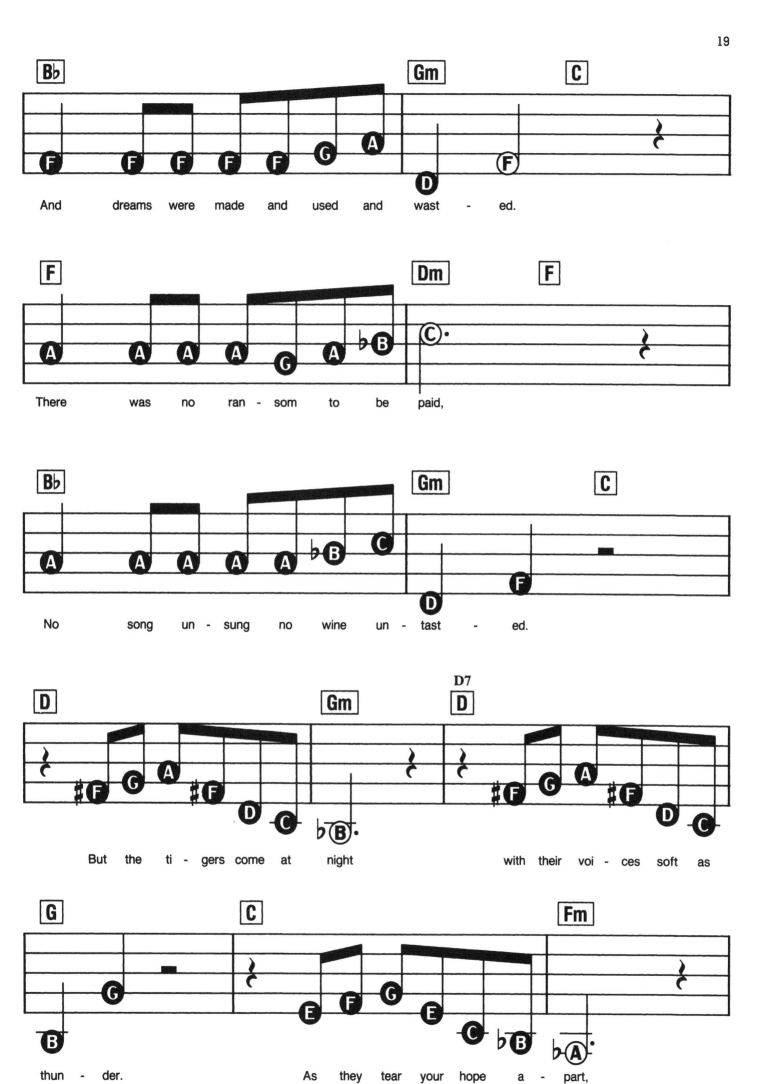

20

D.C. al Coda
(Return to beginning
Play to ✛ and
skip to Coda)

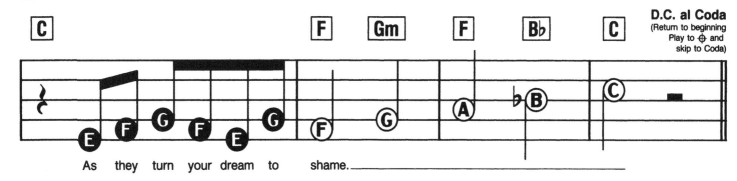

As they turn your dream to shame._____

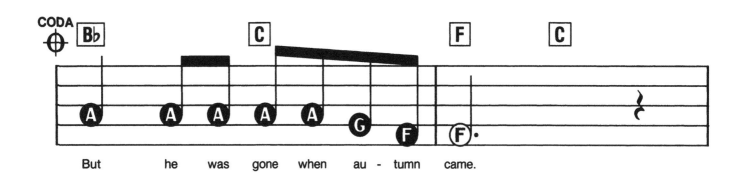

But he was gone when au - tumn came.

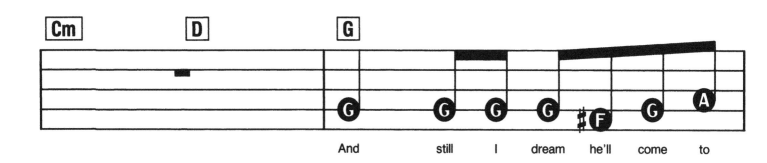

And still I dream he'll come to

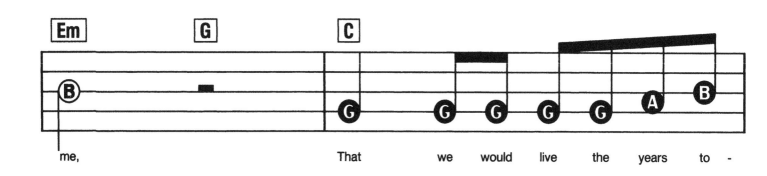

me, That we would live the years to -

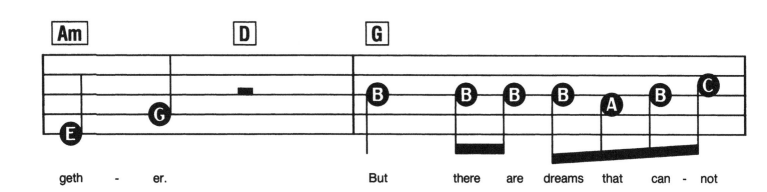

geth - er. But there are dreams that can - not

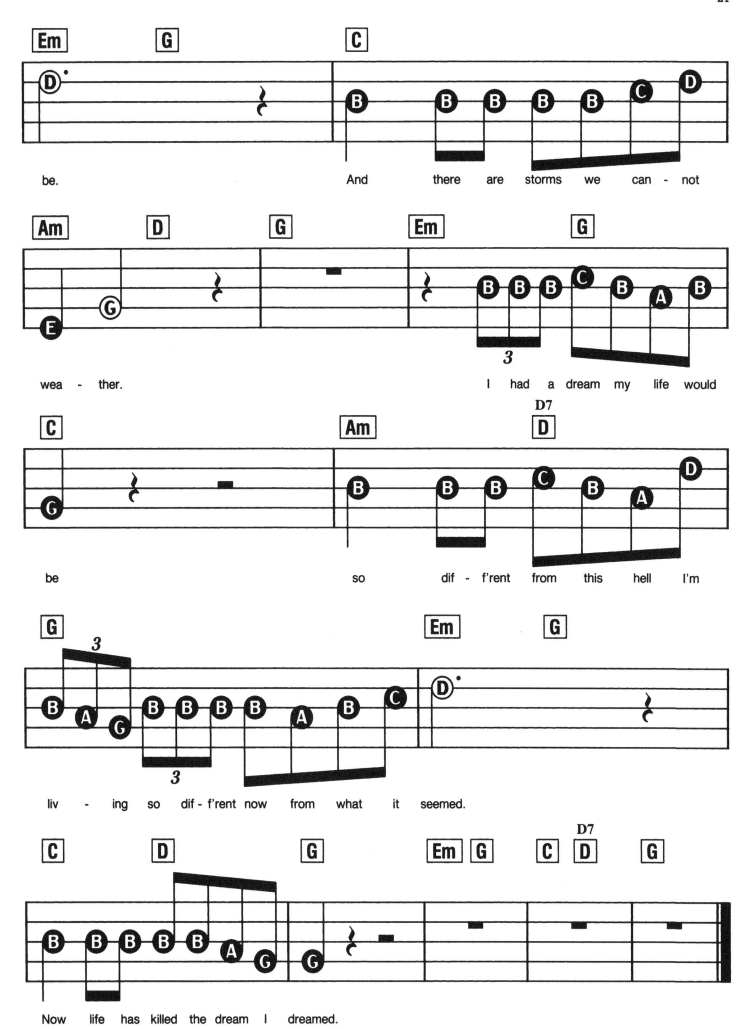

Em G C
be. And there are storms we can - not
Am D G Em G
wea - ther. I had a dream my life would
C Am D7 D
be so dif - f'rent from this hell I'm
G Em G
liv - ing so dif - f'rent now from what it seemed.
C D G Em G C D7 D G
Now life has killed the dream I dreamed.

If I Were a Rich Man
from the Musical FIDDLER ON THE ROOF

Registration 4
Rhythm: March

Words by Sheldon Harnick
Music by Jerry Bock

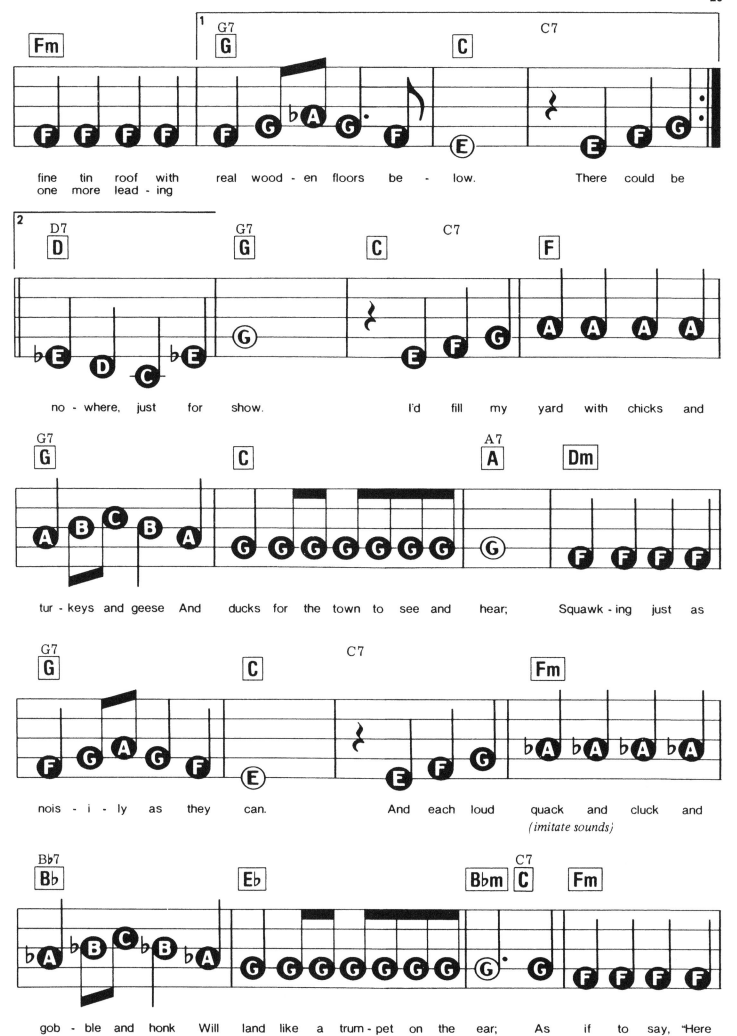

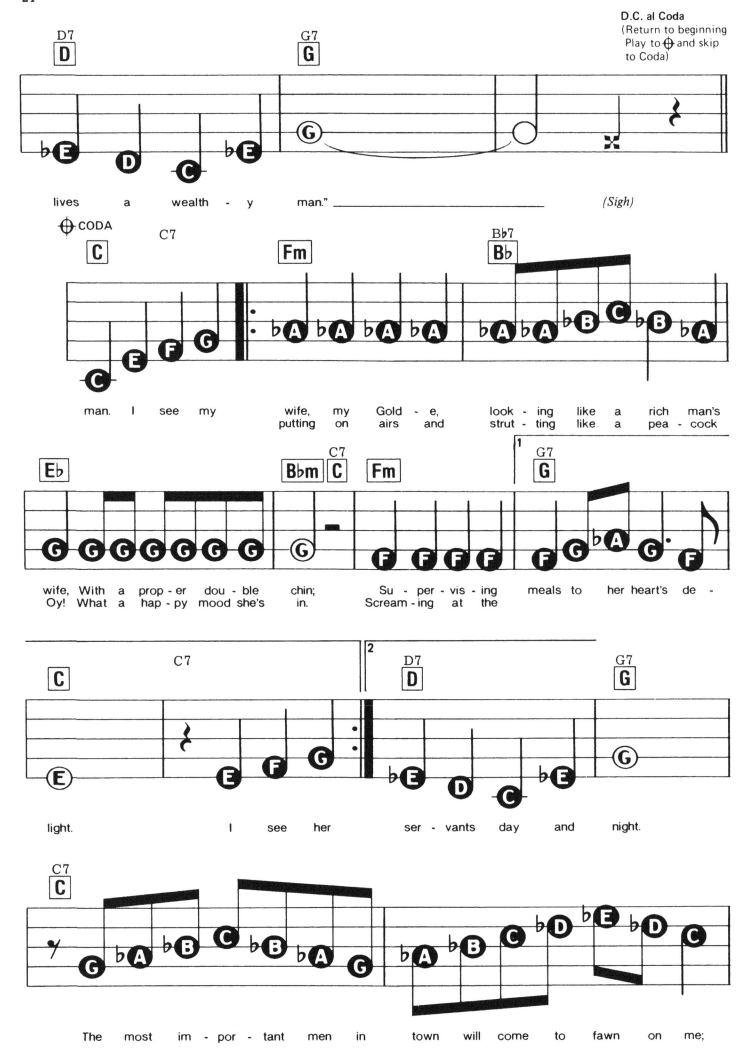

25

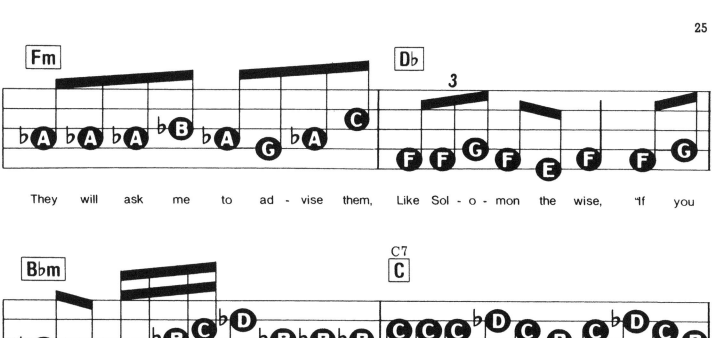

They will ask me to ad - vise them, Like Sol - o - mon the wise, "If you

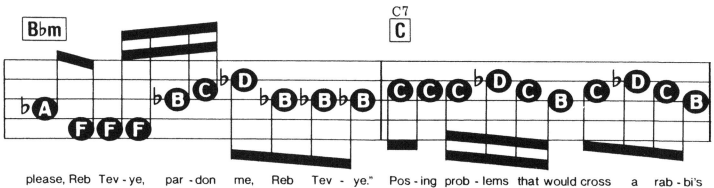

please, Reb Tev - ye, par - don me, Reb Tev - ye." Pos - ing prob - lems that would cross a rab - bi's

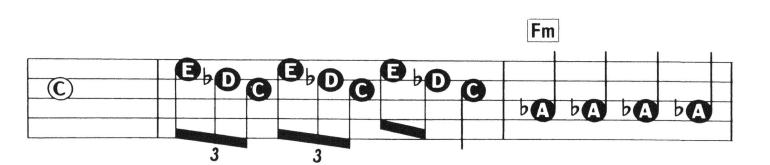

eyes. Boi, boi, boi. boi, boi, boi, boi, boi, boi. And it won't make

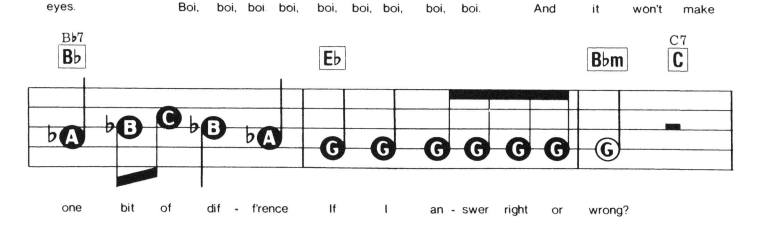

one bit of dif - f'rence If I an - swer right or wrong?

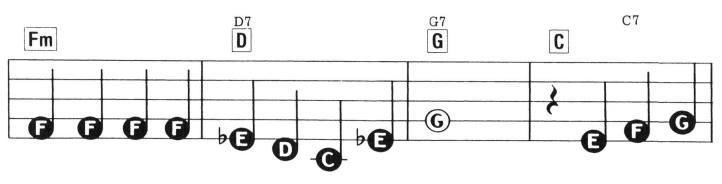

When you're rich, they think you real - ly know. If I were

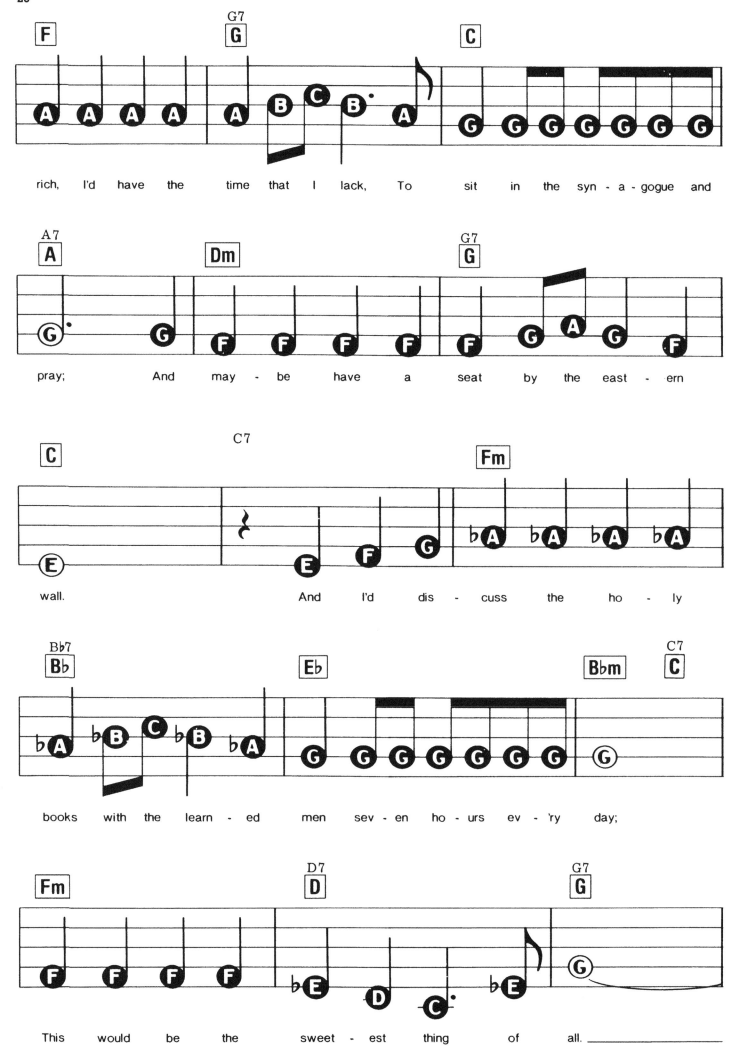

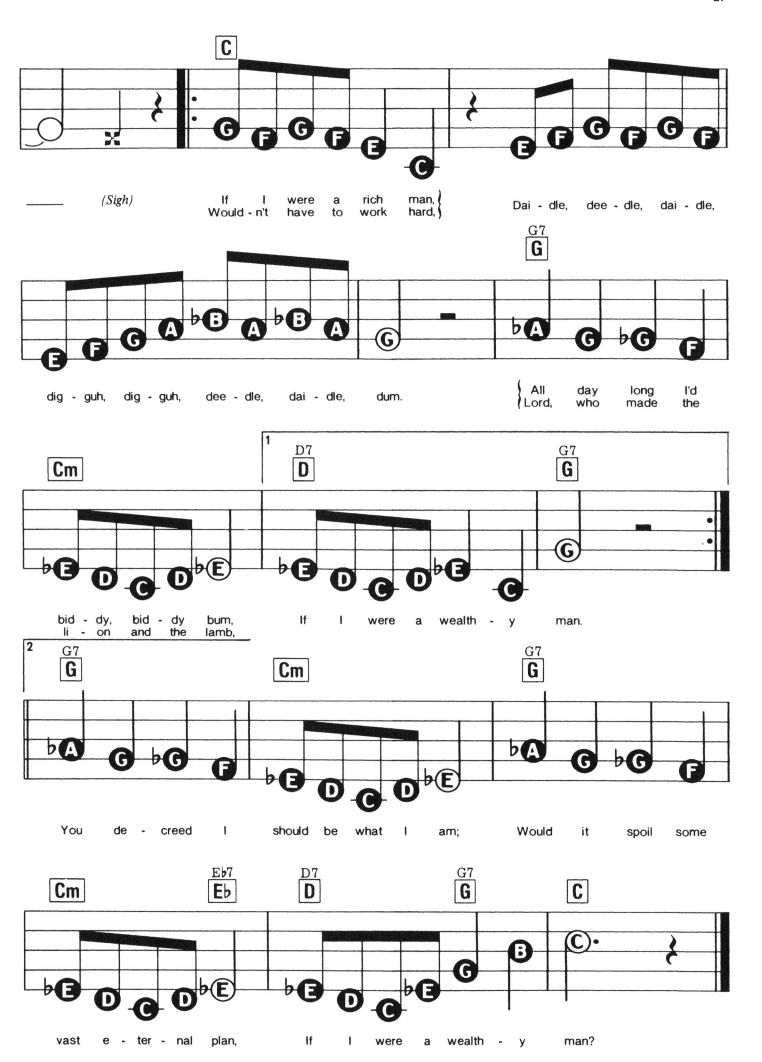

Mame
from MAME

Registration 5
Rhythm: Swing

Music and Lyric by
Jerry Herman

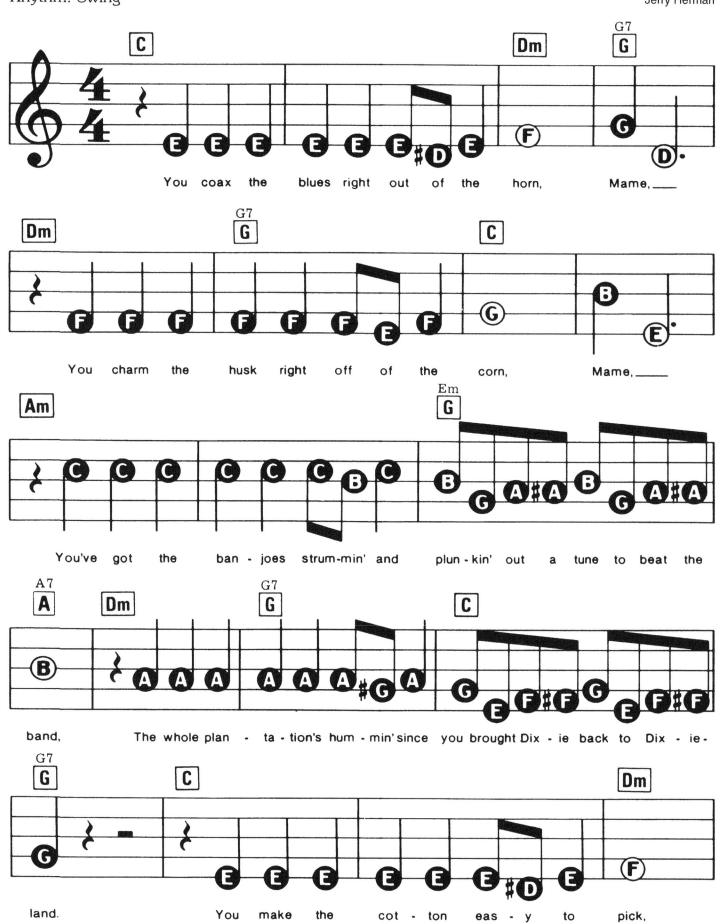

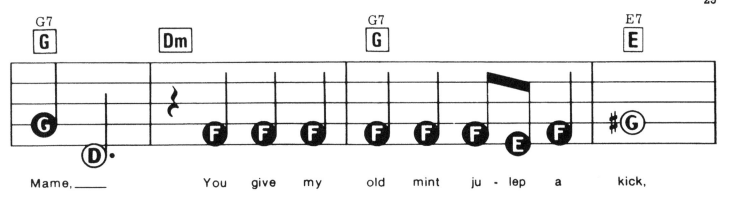

Mame,_____ You give my old mint ju-lep a kick,

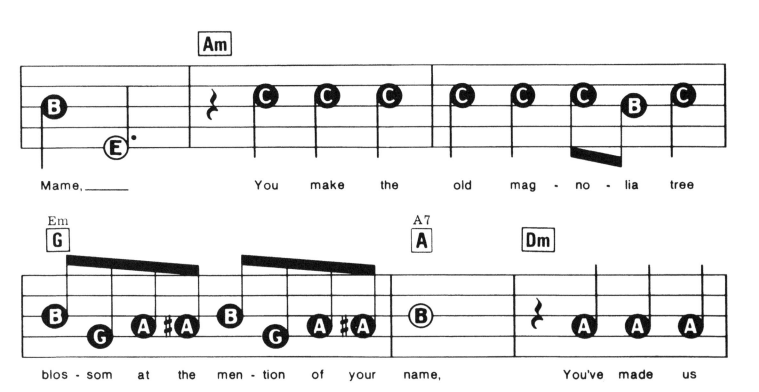

Mame,_____ You make the old mag-no-lia tree

blos-som at the men-tion of your name, You've made us

feel a-live a-gain, You've giv-en us the drive a-gain,

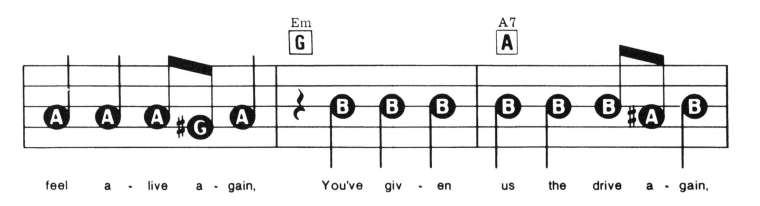

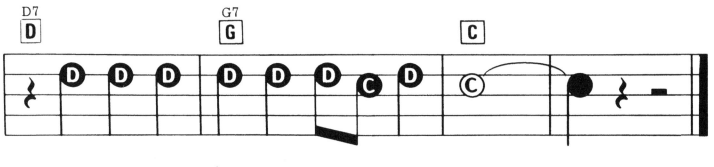

To make the South re-vive a-gain, Mame._____

Mamma Mia
featured in MAMMA MIA!

Registration 3
Rhythm: Rock

Words and Music by Benny Andersson,
Björn Ulvaeus and Stig Anderson

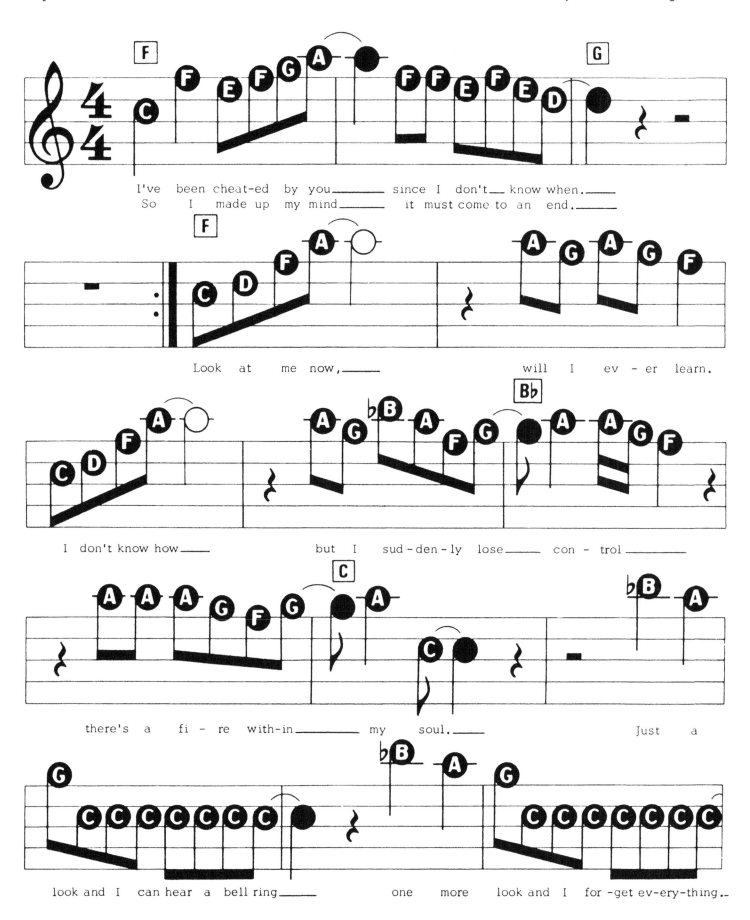

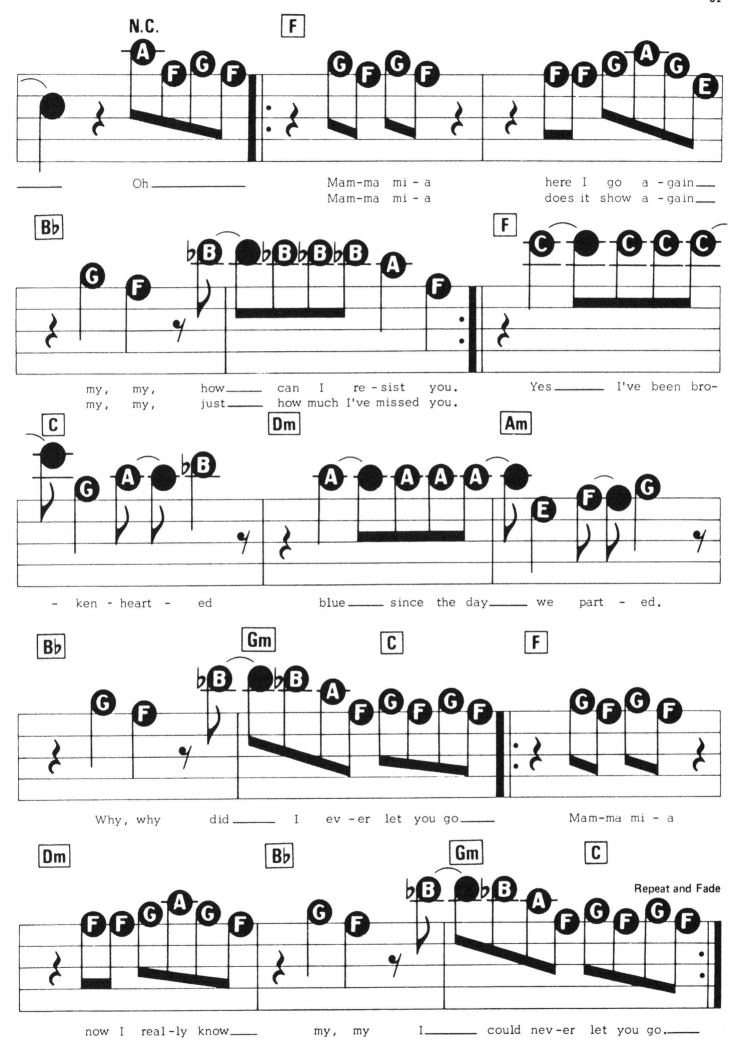

Manhattan
from the Broadway Musical THE GARRICK GAIETIES

Registration 7
Rhythm: Fox Trot

Words by Lorenz Hart
Music by Richard Rodgers

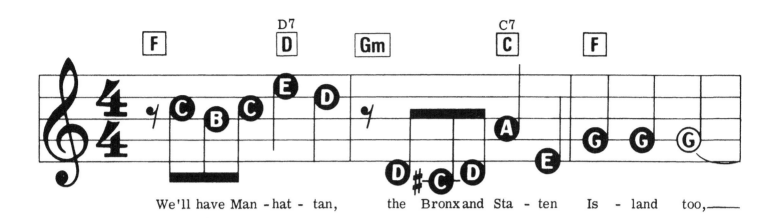

We'll have Man - hat - tan, the Bronx and Sta - ten Is - land too,_____

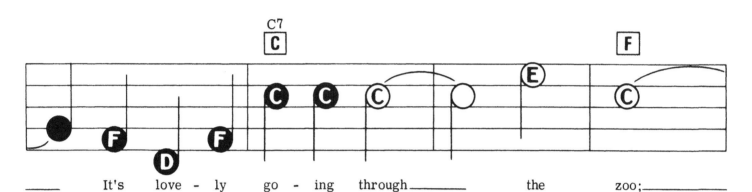

_____ It's love - ly go - ing through_____ the zoo;_____

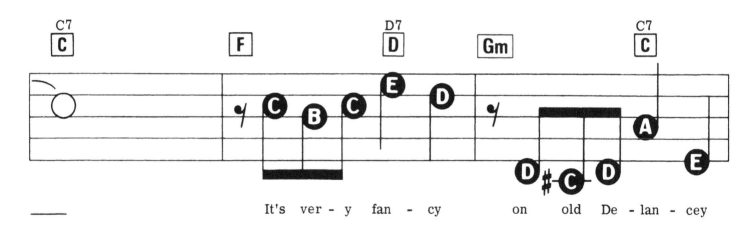

_____ It's ver - y fan - cy on old De - lan - cey

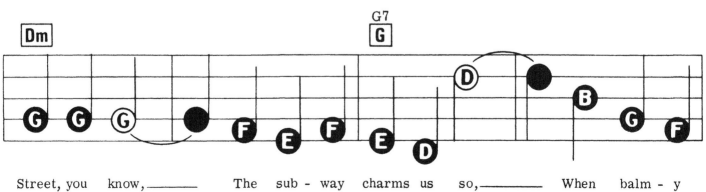

Street, you know,_____ The sub - way charms us so,_____ When balm - y

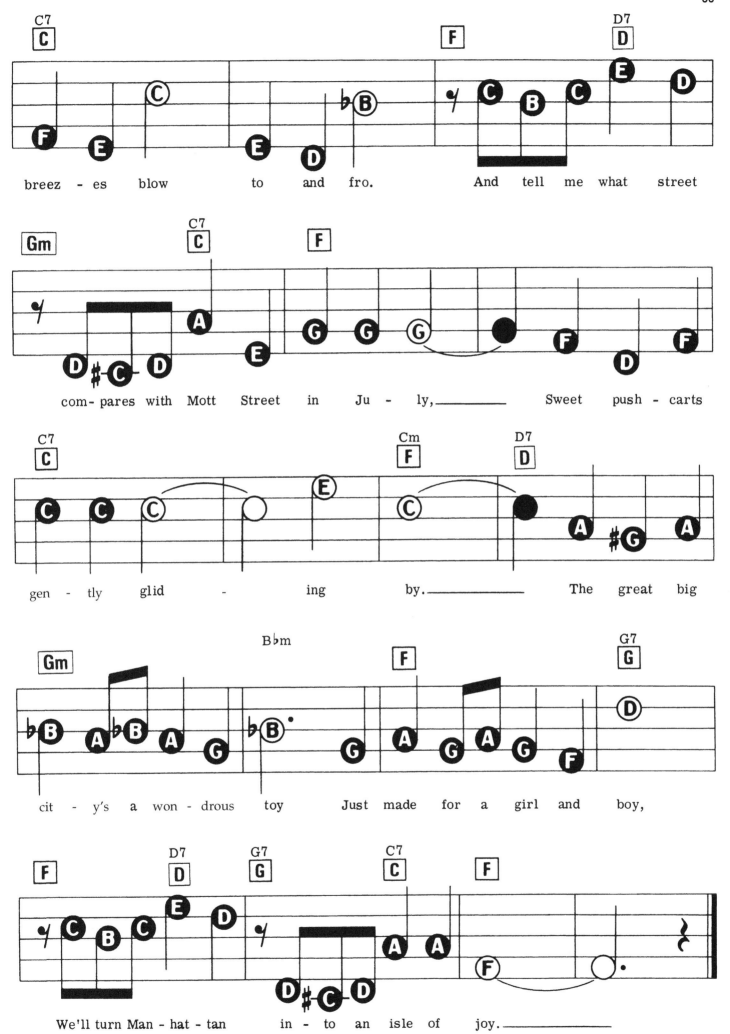

One
from A CHORUS LINE

Registration 5
Rhythm: Fox Trot or Swing

Music by Marvin Hamlisch
Lyric by Edward Kleban

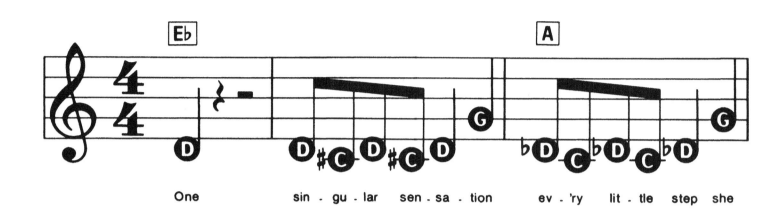

One sin - gu - lar sen - sa - tion ev - 'ry lit - tle step she

takes, One thrill - ing com - bi - na - tion Ev - 'ry move that she

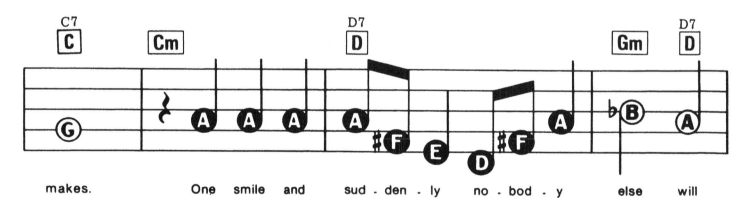

makes. One smile and sud - den - ly no - bod - y else will

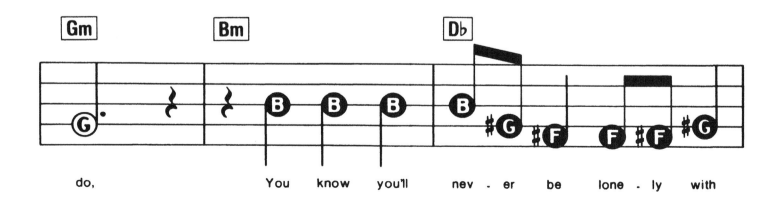

do, You know you'll nev - er be lone - ly with

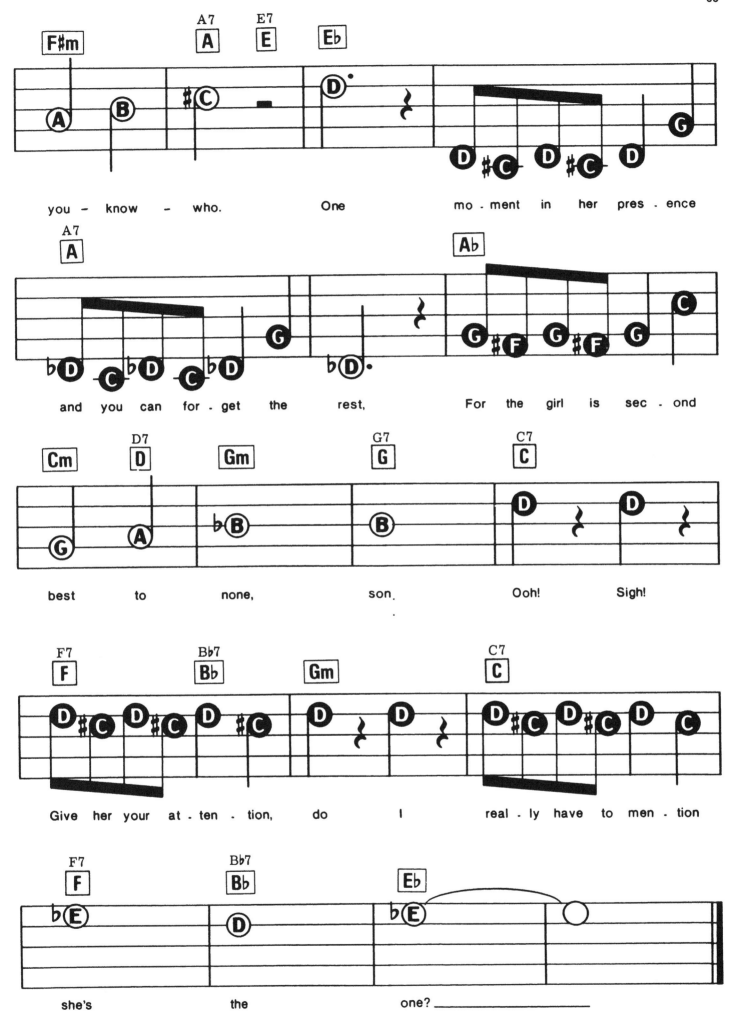

Sixteen Going on Seventeen
from THE SOUND OF MUSIC

Registration 8
Rhythm: Fox Trot or Swing

Lyrics by Oscar Hammerstein II
Music by Richard Rodgers

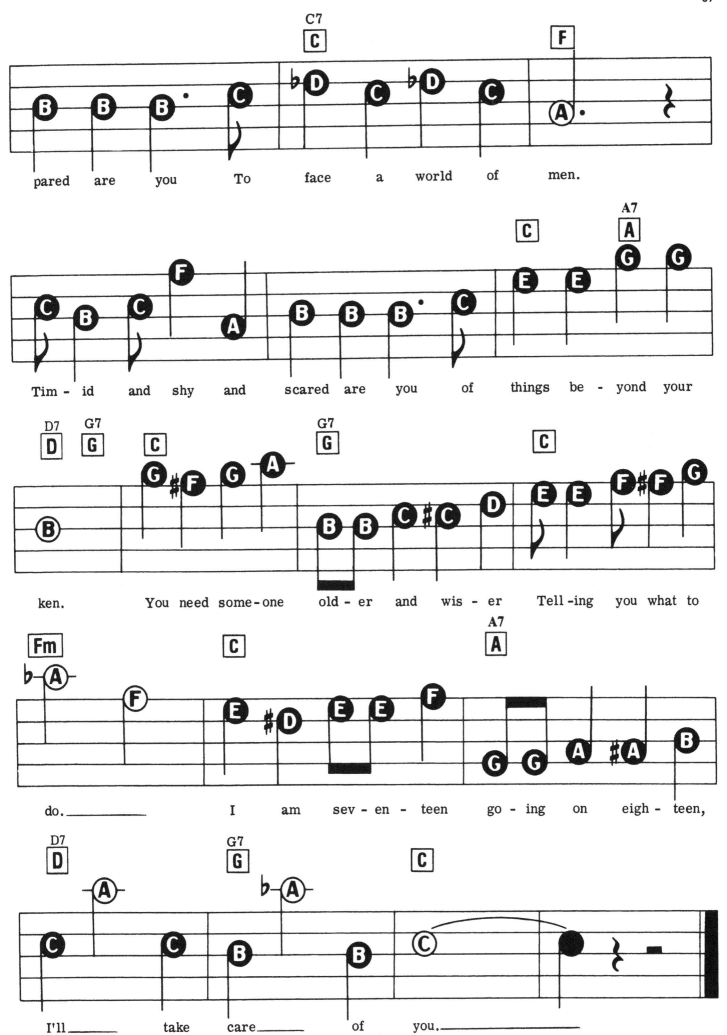

The Sound of Music
from THE SOUND OF MUSIC

Registration 5
Rhythm: Fox Trot

Lyrics by Oscar Hammerstein II
Music by Richard Rodgers

The hills are a - live with the sound of mu - sic,___
hills fill my heart with the sound of mu - sic,___
go to the hills when my heart is lone - ly.___

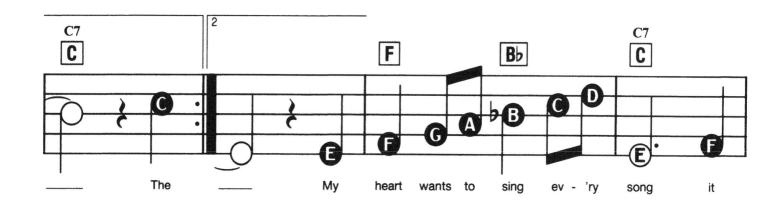

___ With songs they have sung for a thou - sand years.___
I know I will hear what I've heard be - fore.___

The ___ My heart wants to sing ev - 'ry song it

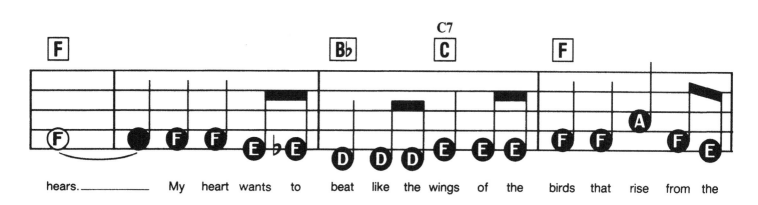

hears.___ My heart wants to beat like the wings of the birds that rise from the

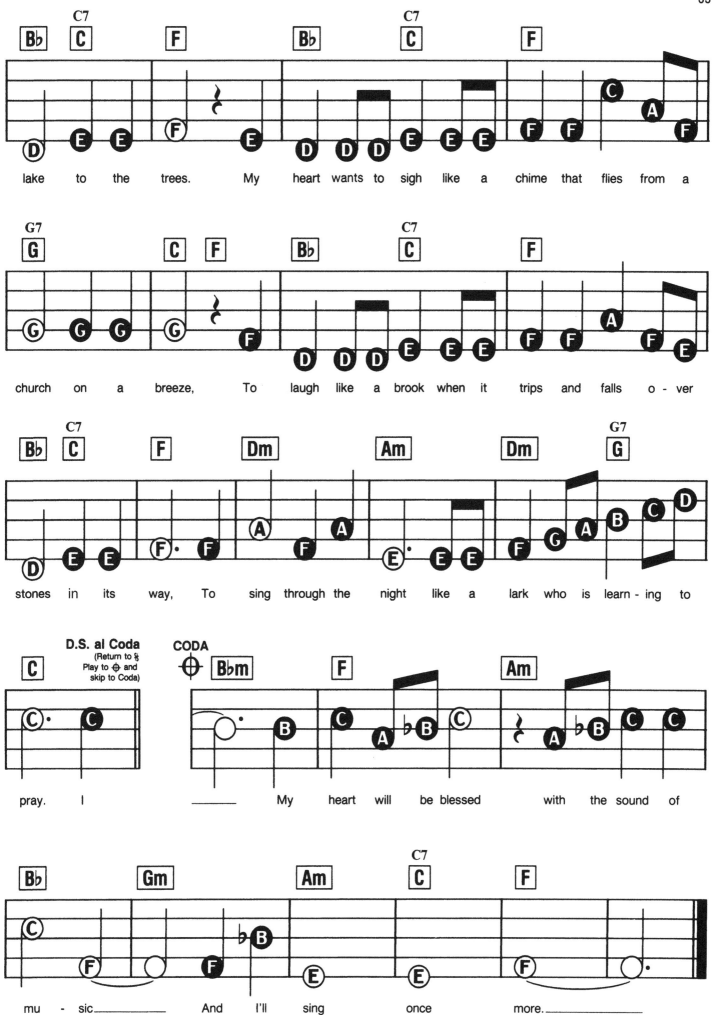

Sunrise, Sunset
from the Musical FIDDLER ON THE ROOF

Registration 1
Rhythm: Waltz

Words by Sheldon Harnick
Music by Jerry Bock

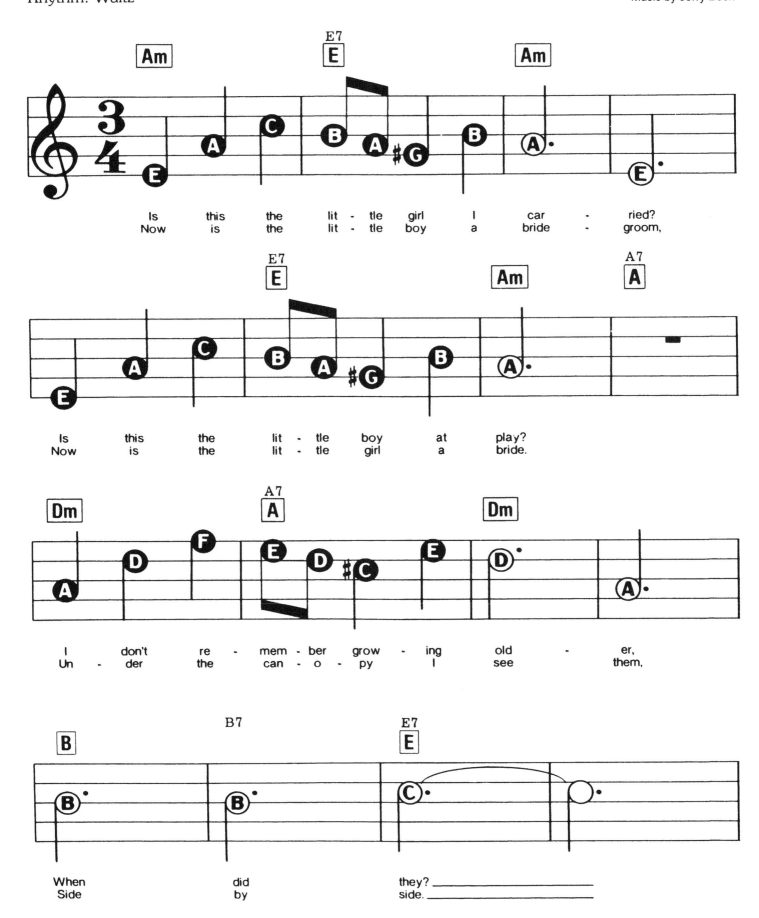

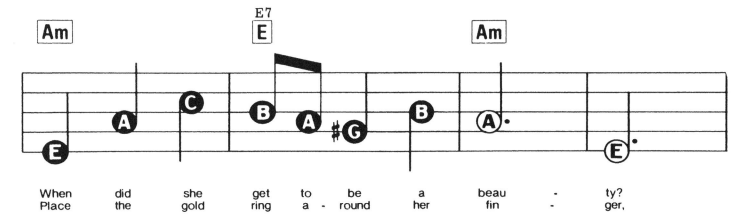

When did she get to be a beau - ty?
Place the gold ring a - round her fin - ger,

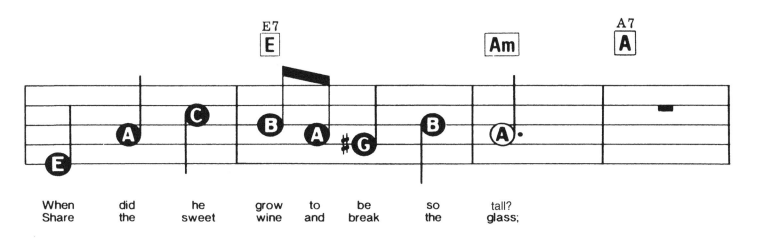

When did he grow to be so tall?
Share the sweet wine and break the glass;

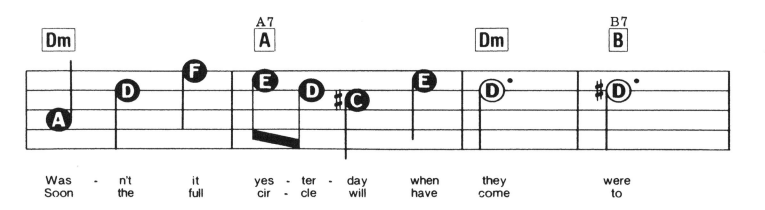

Was - n't it yes - ter - day when they were
Soon the full cir - cle will have come to

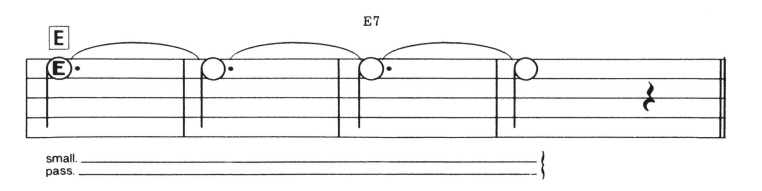

small. _____
pass. _____

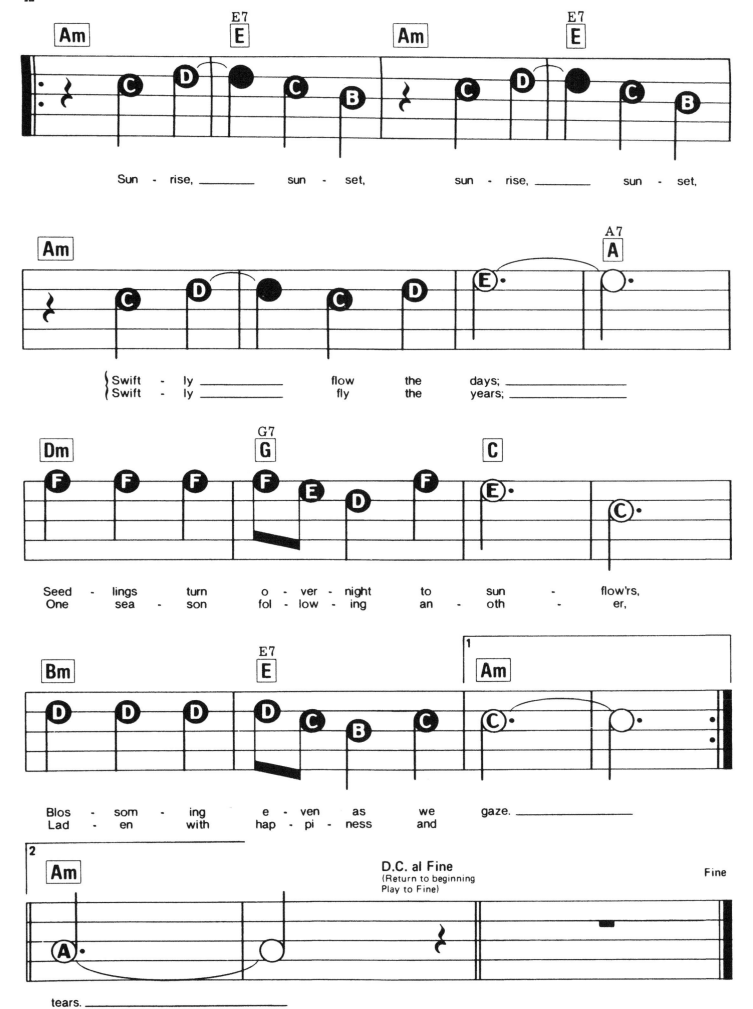

Sun - rise, _____ sun - set, sun - rise, _____ sun - set,

Swift - ly _____ flow the days; _____
Swift - ly _____ fly the years; _____

Seed - lings turn o - ver - night to sun - flow'rs,
One sea - son fol - low - ing an - oth - er,

Blos - som - ing e - ven as we gaze. _____
Lad - en with hap - pi - ness and

D.C. al Fine
(Return to beginning
Play to Fine)

Fine

tears. _____

A Wonderful Day Like Today
from THE ROAR OF THE GREASEPAINT - THE SMELL OF THE CROWD

Registration 1
Rhythm: Fox Trot

Words and Music by Leslie Bricusse
and Anthony Newley

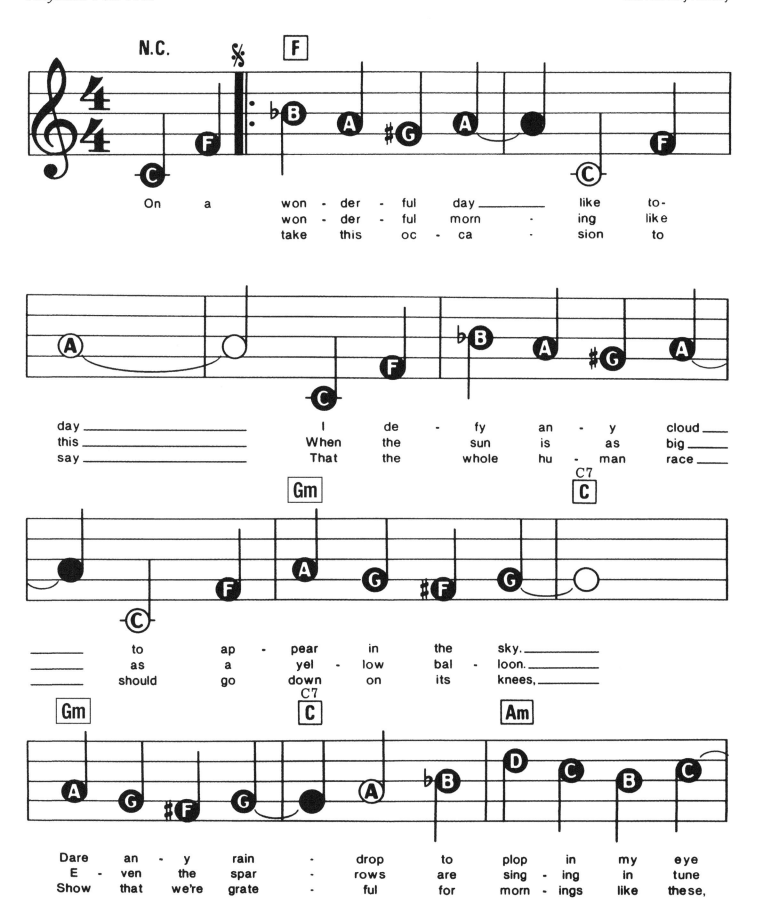

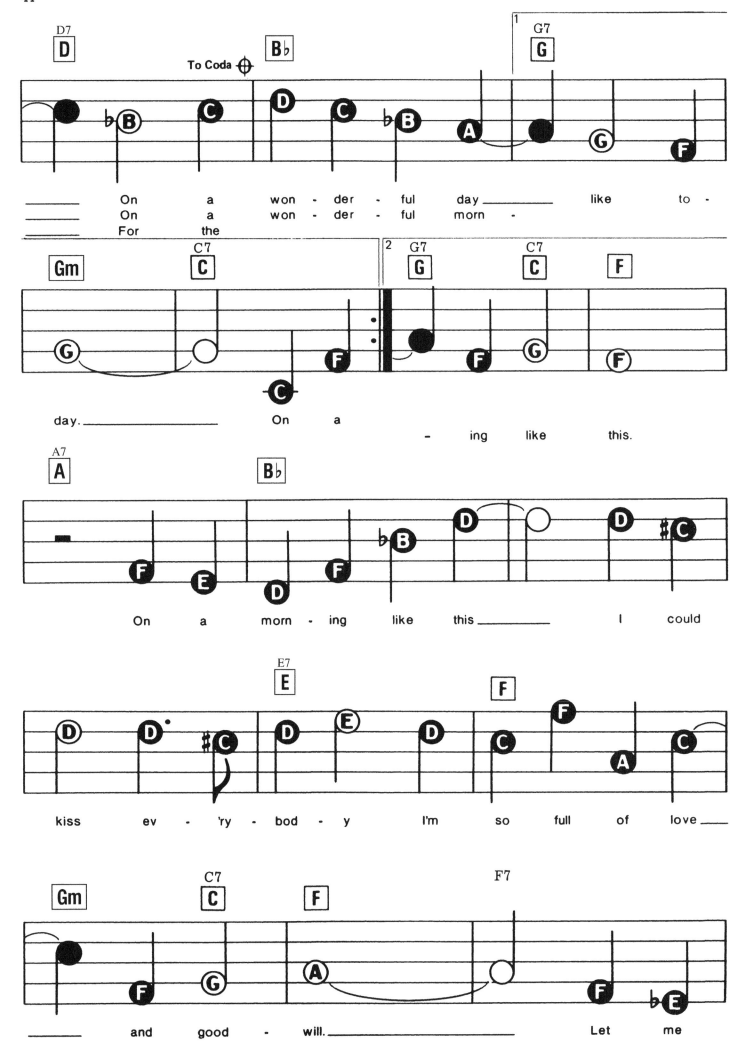

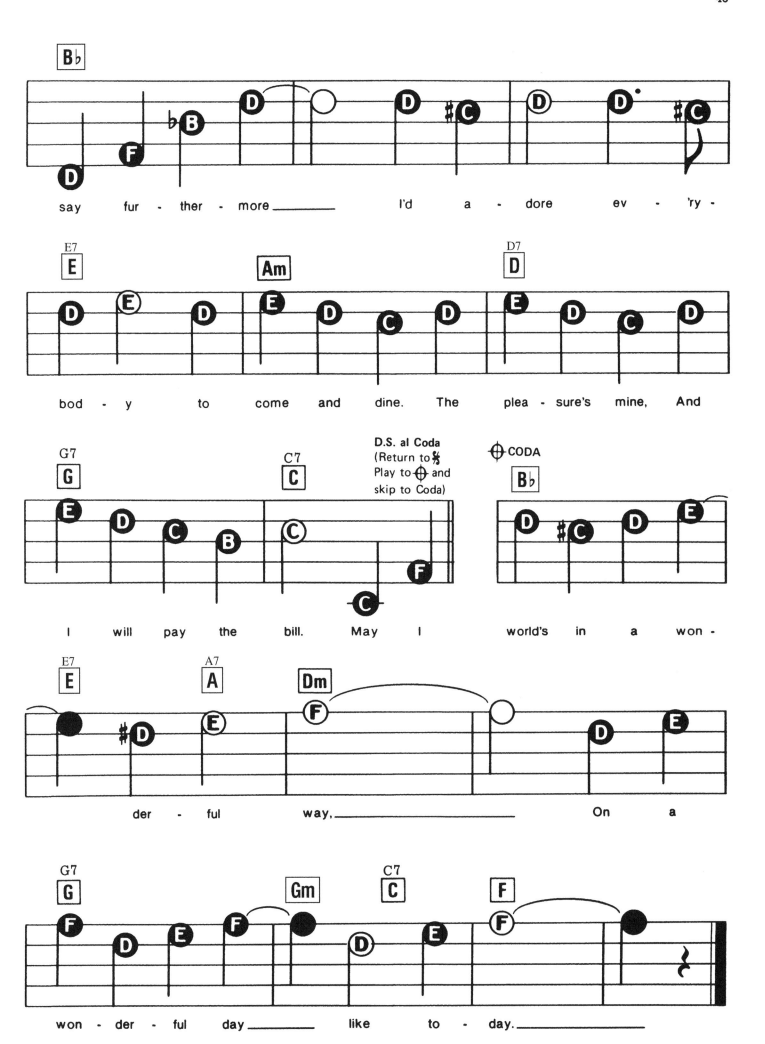

There's No Business Like Show Business

from the Stage Production ANNIE GET YOUR GUN

Registration 2
Rhythm: Fox Trot

Words and Music by
Irving Berlin

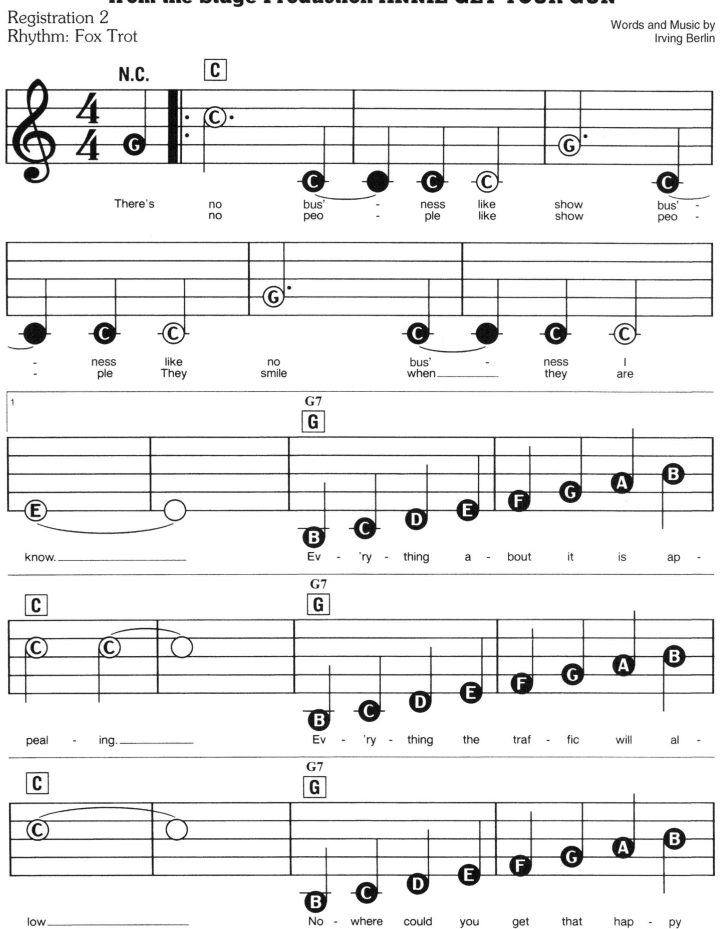

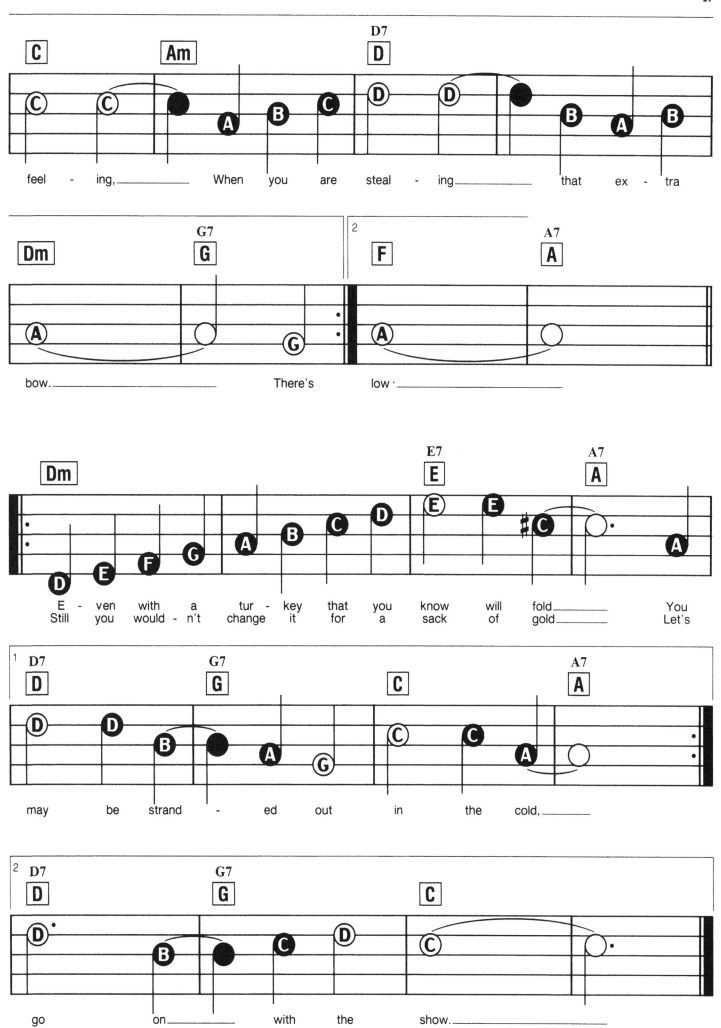

This Nearly Was Mine

from SOUTH PACIFIC

Registration 3
Rhythm: Waltz

Lyrics by Oscar Hammerstein II
Music by Richard Rodgers

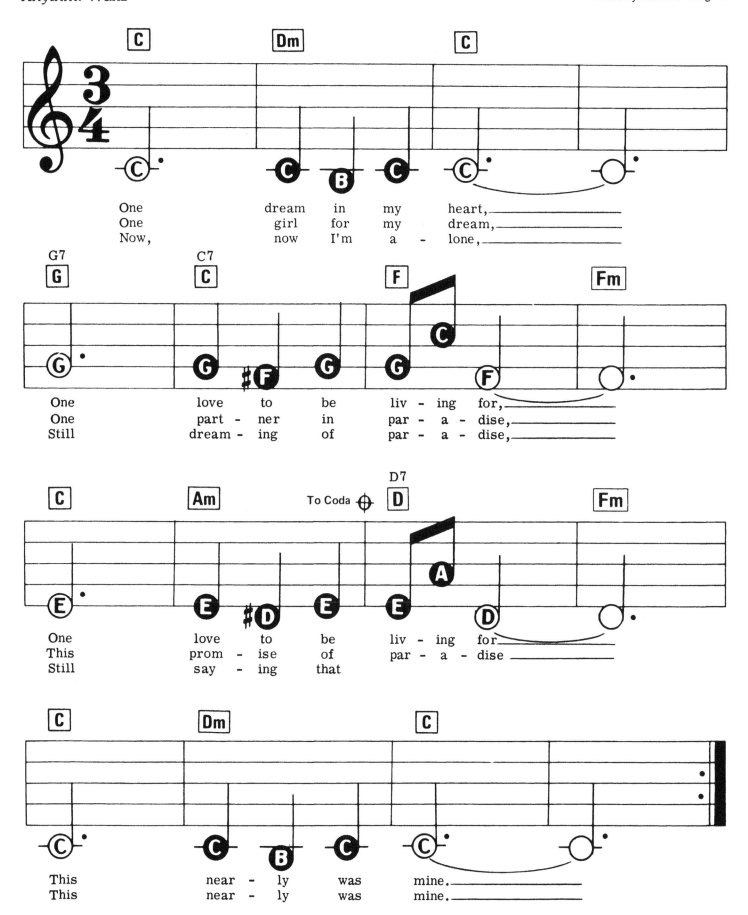

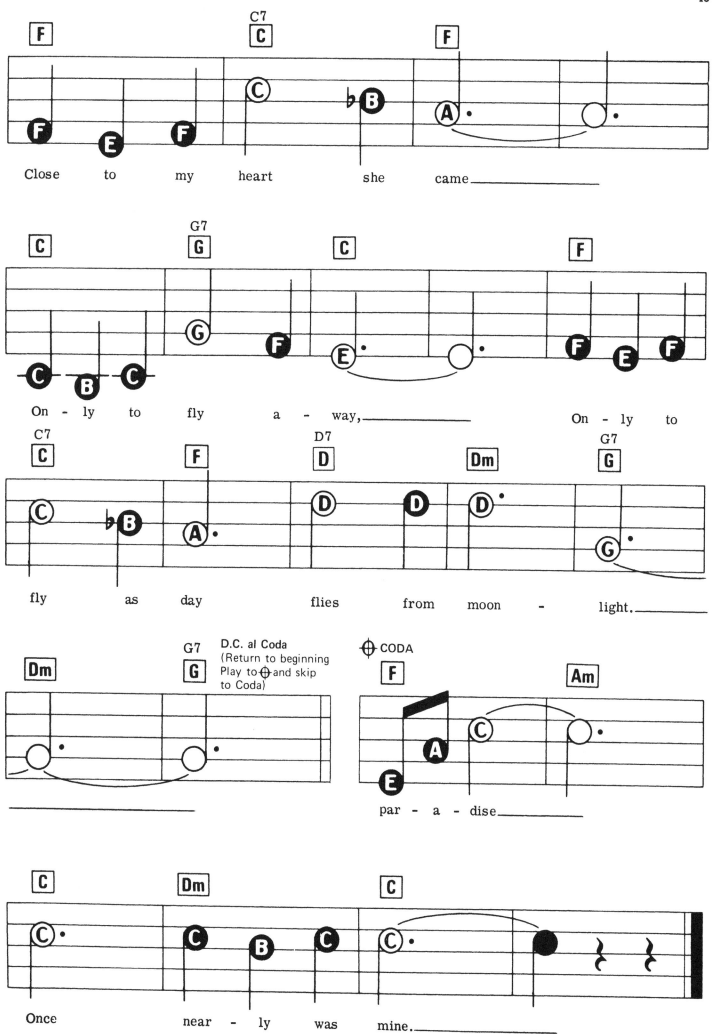

Tomorrow
from the Musical Production ANNIE

Registration 1
Rhythm: Swing or Jazz

Lyric by Martin Charnin
Music by Charles Strouse

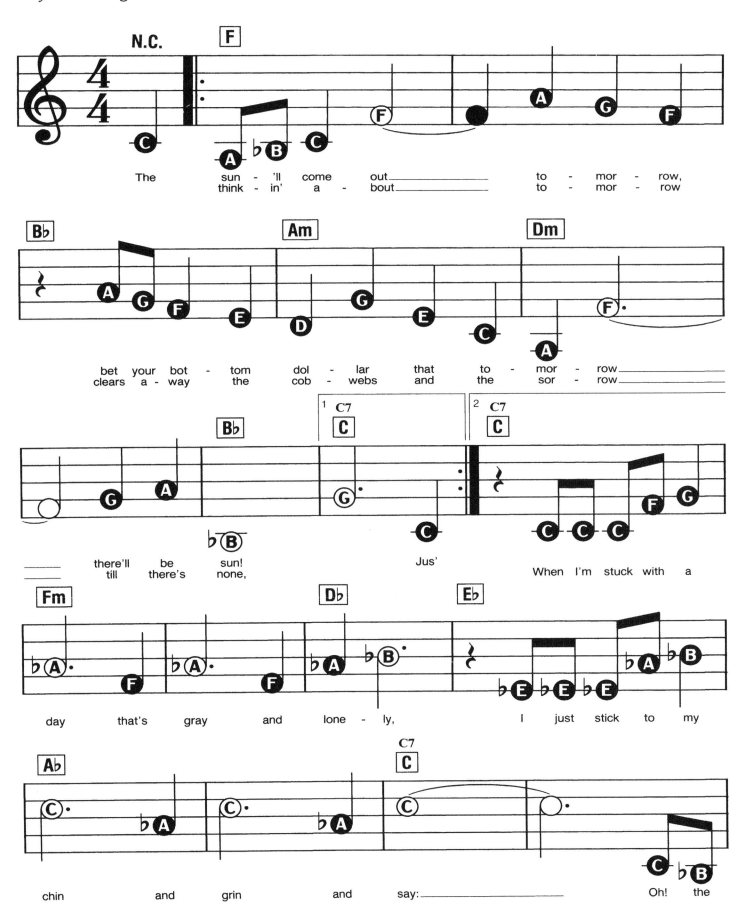

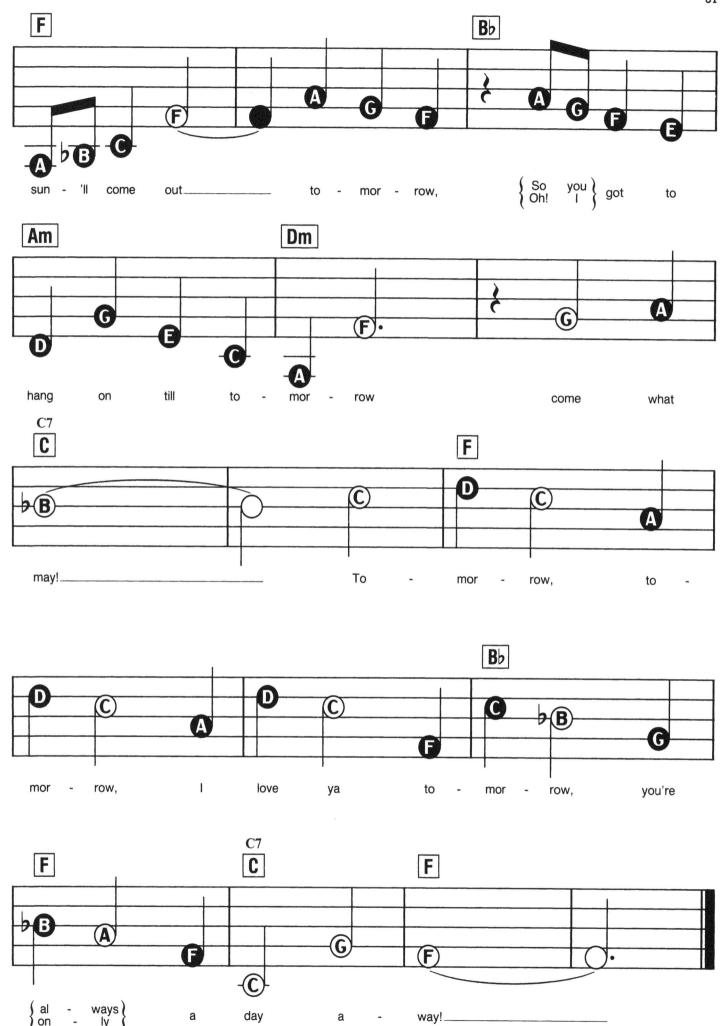

What I Did for Love
from A CHORUS LINE

Registration 3
Rhythm: Ballad

Music by Marvin Hamlisch
Lyric by Edward Kleban

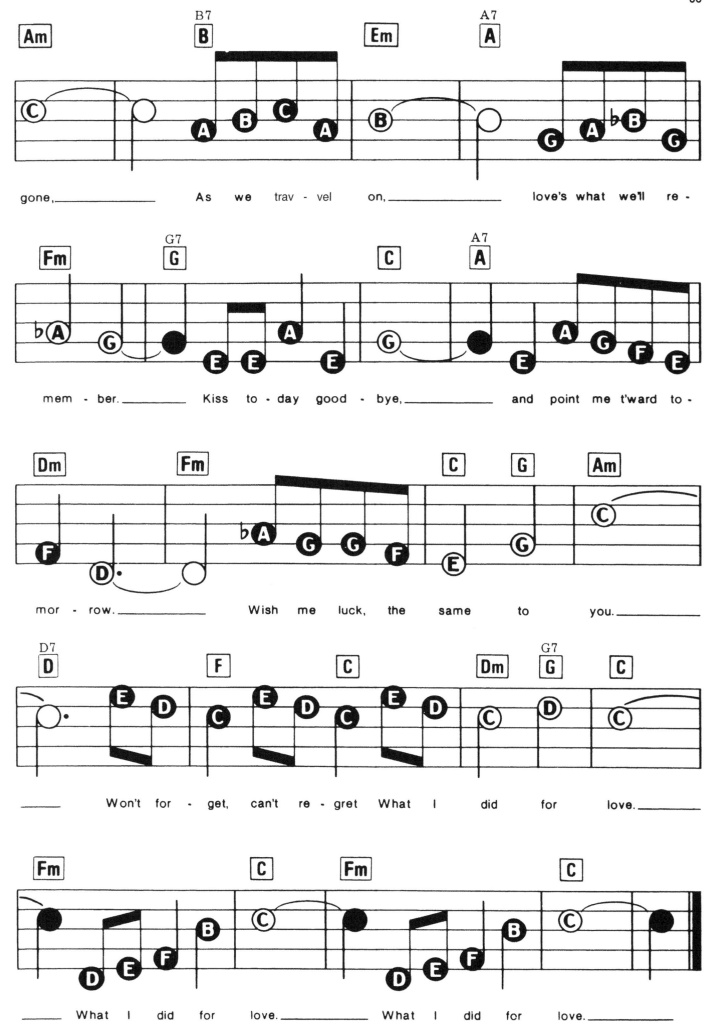

Who Can I Turn To
(When Nobody Needs Me)
from THE ROAR OF THE GREASEPAINT - THE SMELL OF THE CROWD

Registration 10
Rhythm: Ballad or Fox Trot

Words and Music by Leslie Bricusse
and Anthony Newley

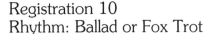

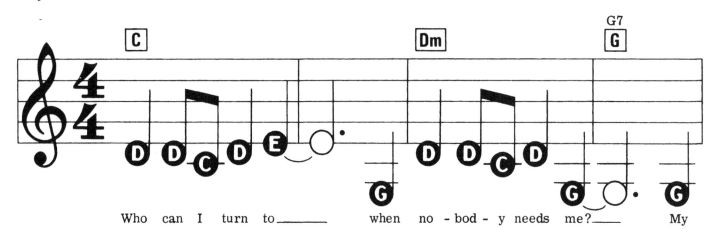

Who can I turn to_____ when no-bod-y needs me?_____ My

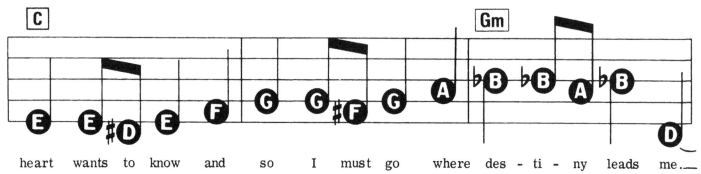

heart wants to know and so I must go where des-ti-ny leads me.__

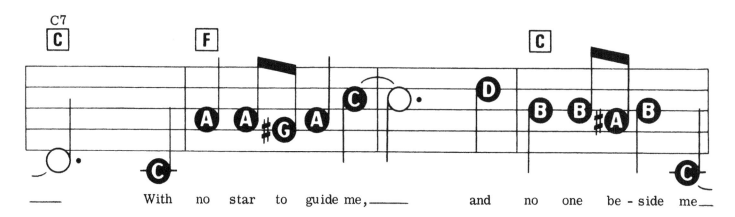

__ With no star to guide me,_____ and no one be-side me__

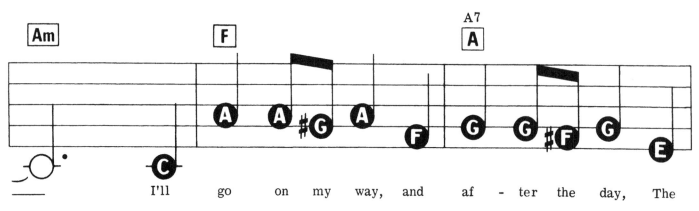

__ I'll go on my way, and af-ter the day, The

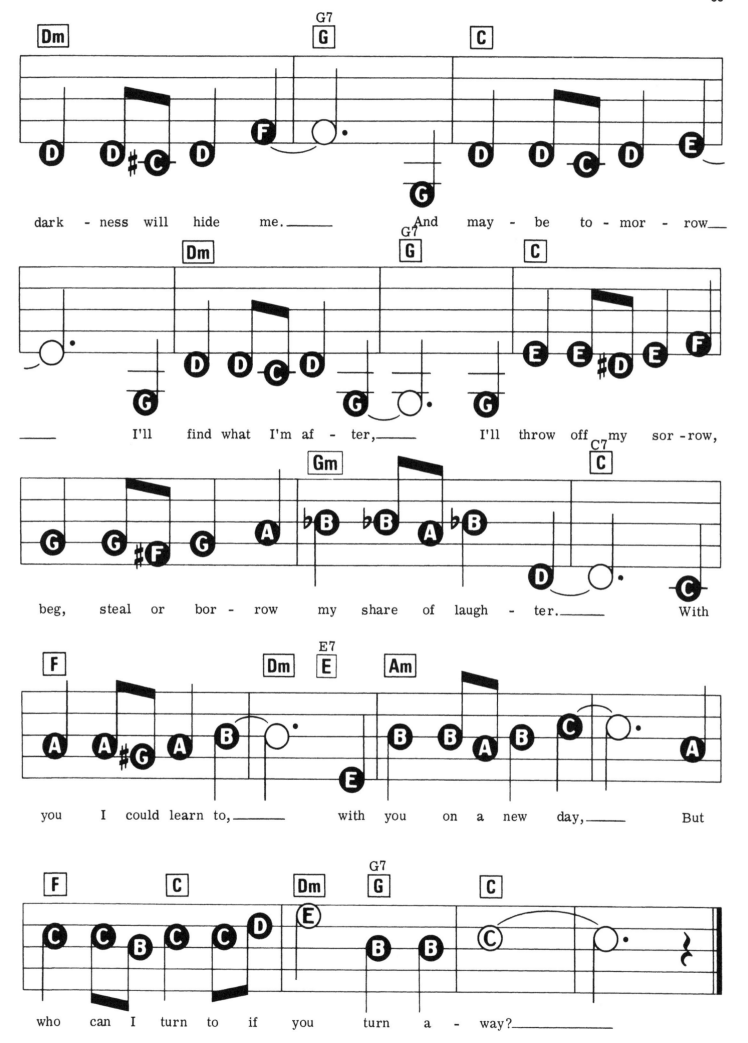

Registration Guide

- Match the Registration number on the song to the corresponding numbered category below. Select and activate an instrumental sound available on your instrument.

- Choose an automatic rhythm appropriate to the mood and style of the song. (Consult your Owner's Guide for proper operation of automatic rhythm features.)

- Adjust the tempo and volume controls to comfortable settings.

Registration

1	Mellow	Flutes, Clarinet, Oboe, Flugel Horn, Trombone, French Horn, Organ Flutes
2	Ensemble	Brass Section, Sax Section, Wind Ensemble, Full Organ, Theater Organ
3	Strings	Violin, Viola, Cello, Fiddle, String Ensemble, Pizzicato, Organ Strings
4	Guitars	Acoustic/Electric Guitars, Banjo, Mandolin, Dulcimer, Ukulele, Hawaiian Guitar
5	Mallets	Vibraphone, Marimba, Xylophone, Steel Drums, Bells, Celesta, Chimes
6	Liturgical	Pipe Organ, Hand Bells, Vocal Ensemble, Choir, Organ Flutes
7	Bright	Saxophones, Trumpet, Mute Trumpet, Synth Leads, Jazz/Gospel Organs
8	Piano	Piano, Electric Piano, Honky Tonk Piano, Harpsichord, Clavi
9	Novelty	Melodic Percussion, Wah Trumpet, Synth, Whistle, Kazoo, Perc. Organ
10	Bellows	Accordion, French Accordion, Mussette, Harmonica, Pump Organ, Bagpipes